CROCHET

Pineapples Through the Home™

Many of the products used in this pattern book can be purchased from local craft, fabric and variety stores, or from the Annie's Attic Needlecraft Catalog *(see Customer Service information on page 47).*

Contents

Pineapple Lampshade Cover 3

Pineapple Angel 6

Pineapple Afghan..................... 10

Round Tablecloth 13

Small Pineapple Doily 18

Songbird Wreath 20

Small Pineapple Basket..................... 22

Tissue Box Cover 26

Mirror Image Doily 29

Square Pineapple Doily 32

Pineapple Runner 36

Pineapple Rug..................................40

Pillowcase & Sheet Edgings..............42

Island Ecstasy Runner 44

Stitch Guide 47

Pineapple Lampshade Cover

Design by Jo Ann Maxwell

SKILL LEVEL

INTERMEDIATE

FINISHED SIZE

Fits lampshade 13½ inches tall, 9 inches across top and 16 inches across bottom

MATERIALS

- ❑ Size 10 crochet cotton: 350 yds #462 natural
- ❑ Size F/5/3.75mm crochet hook or size needed to obtain gauge
- ❑ Sewing needle
- ❑ Matching sewing thread
- ❑ Cloth or vinyl lampshade 13½ inches tall, 9 inches across top and 16 inches across bottom
- ❑ Plastic wrap
- ❑ 1½ yds ⅜-wide light green satin ribbon
- ❑ 16 rose-colored 1-inch gathered ribbon roses with leaves

GAUGE

34 dc = 5 inches

PATTERN NOTES

Join with slip stitch as indicated unless otherwise stated.

Chain-3 at beginning of row or round counts as first double crochet unless otherwise stated.

SPECIAL STITCHES

Beginning shell (beg shell): Ch 3, (dc, ch 2, 2 dc) in place indicated.

Shell: (2 dc, ch 2, 2 dc) in place indicated.

Picot: Ch 3, sl st in last sc.

Beginning double shell (beg double shell): (Beg shell, ch 2, 2 dc) in place indicated.

Double shell: (Shell, ch 2, 2 dc) in place indicated.

INSTRUCTIONS
LAMPSHADE COVER

Rnd 1: Ch 192, sl st in first ch to form ring, ch 5 *(counts as first dc and ch-2)*, sk next 2 chs, dc in next ch, ch 2, [sk next 2 chs, dc in next ch, ch 2] around, **join** *(see Pattern Notes)* in 3rd ch of beg ch-5. *(64 dc, 64 ch-2 sps)*

Rnd 2: Ch 3 *(see Pattern Notes)*, dc in each dc and each ch around, join in 3rd ch of beg ch-3. *(192 dc)*

Rnd 3: Beg shell *(see Special Stitches)* in first st, [ch 2, sk next 5 sts, **shell** *(see Special Stitches)* in next st] around, ending with hdc in 3rd ch of beg ch-3 to form last ch-2 sp. *(32 shells)*

Rnd 4: Sl st in ch sp just formed, ch 1, [sc, ch 7, sc] in same ch sp, [ch 7, sk next shell, (sc, ch 7, sc) in next ch-2 sp] around, ending with ch 3, tr in beg sc, forming last ch sp. *(64 ch-7 sps)*

Rnds 5–25: Ch 1, sc in ch sp just formed, [ch 7, sc in next ch-7 sp] around, ending with ch 3, tr in beg sc, forming last ch sp.

Rnd 26: Beg shell in ch sp just formed, *ch 3, (sc, **picot**—*see Special Stitches*) in next ch-7 sp, ch 3**, shell in 4th ch of next ch-7, rep from * around, ending last rep at **, join in 3rd ch of beg ch-3. *(32 shells)*

Rnd 27: Sl st in next dc and in ch-2 sp, beg shell in same ch sp, *ch 3, 2 dc in first dc of next shell, dc in next dc, 6 dc in ch-2 sp of next shell, dc in next dc, 2 dc in next dc, ch 3**, shell in ch-2 sp of next shell, rep from * around, ending last rep at **, join in 3rd ch of beg ch-3.

Rnd 28: Sl st in next dc and in ch-2 sp, beg shell in same ch sp, *ch 3, sc in next ch-3 sp, [dc in next dc, ch 1] 11 times, dc in next dc, sc in next ch-3 sp, ch 3**, shell in ch-2 sp of next shell, rep from * around, ending last rep at **, join in 3rd ch of beg ch-3.

Rnd 29: Sl st in next dc and in ch-2 sp, beg shell in same ch sp, *ch 3, sk next ch-3 sp, [sc in next dc, ch 3] 12 times**, shell in ch-2 sp of next shell, rep from * around, ending last rep at **, join in 3rd ch of beg ch-3.

Rnd 30: Sl st in next dc and in ch-2 sp, beg shell in same ch sp, *ch 3, sk next ch-3 sp, [sc in next ch-3 sp, ch 3] 11 times**, shell in ch-2 sp of next shell, rep from * around, ending last rep at **, join in 3rd ch of beg ch-3.

Rnd 31: Sl st in next dc and in ch-2 sp, **beg double shell** *(see Special Stitches)* in same ch sp, ch 3, sk next ch-3 sp, [sc in next ch-3 sp, ch 3] 10 times**, **double shell** *(see Special Stitches)* in ch-2 sp of next shell, rep from * around, ending last rep at **, join in 3rd ch of beg ch-3.

Rnd 32: Sl st in next dc and in ch-2 sp, beg shell in same ch sp, shell in next ch-2 sp, *ch 3, sk next ch-3 sp, [sc in next ch-3 sp, ch 3] 9 times**, shell in each of next 2 ch-2 sps, rep from * around, ending last rep at **, join in 3rd ch of beg ch-3.

Rnd 33: Sl st in next dc and in ch-2 sp, ch 1, shell in ch-2 sp of next shell, *ch 3, sk next ch-3 sp, [sc in next ch-3 sp, ch 3] 8 times**, shell in ch-2 sp of next shell, ch 1, shell in ch-2 sp of next shell, rep from * around, ending last rep at **, join in 3rd ch of beg ch-3. Fasten off.

First Pineapple

Row 34: Join with sl st in unworked ch sp of first shell of rnd 33 to the right of next pineapple, beg shell in same ch sp, ch 3, sk next ch-3 sp, [sc in next ch-3 sp, ch 3] 7 times, shell in ch-2 sp of next shell, turn.

Row 35: Ch 3, shell in ch sp of first shell, ch 3, sk next ch-3 sp, [sc in next ch-3 sp, ch 3] 6 times, shell in ch sp of next shell, turn.

Row 36: Ch 3, shell in ch sp of first shell, ch 3, sk next ch-3 sp, [sc in next ch-3 sp, ch 3] 5 times, shell in ch sp of next shell, turn.

Row 37: Ch 3, shell in ch sp of first shell, ch 3, sk next ch-3 sp, [sc in next ch-3 sp, ch 3] 4 times, shell in ch sp of next shell, turn.

Row 38: Ch 3, shell in ch sp of first shell, ch 3, sk next ch-3 sp, [sc in next ch-3 sp, ch 3] 3 times, shell in ch sp of next shell, turn.

Row 39: Ch 3, shell in ch sp of first shell, ch 3, sk next ch-3 sp, [sc in next ch-3 sp, ch 3] twice, shell in ch sp of next shell, turn.

Row 40: Ch 3, shell in ch sp of first shell, ch 3, sk next ch-3 sp, sc in next ch-3 sp, ch 3, shell in ch sp of next shell, turn.

Row 41: Ch 3, shell in ch sp of first shell, shell in ch sp of next shell, ch 3, sl st in first dc of first shell on last row, fasten off.

Next Pineapples

Rows 34–41: Rep Rows 34–41 for each of rem 15 Pineapples.

Top Pineapple Border

Rnd 1: Join with a sl st in ch sp of any shell on rnd 3, beg shell in same ch sp, *ch 2, 7 dc in ch sp of next shell, ch 2**, shell in ch sp of next shell, rep from * around, ending last rep at **, join in 3rd ch of beg ch-3.

Rnd 2: Sl st in next dc and in ch-2 sp, beg shell in same ch sp, *ch 2, sc in next ch-2 sp, [dc in next dc, ch 1] 6 times, dc in next dc, sc in next ch-2 sp, ch 2**, shell in ch sp of next shell, rep from * around, ending last rep at **, join in 3rd ch of beg ch-3.

Rnd 3: Sl st in next dc and in ch-2 sp, beg shell in same ch sp, *ch 3, sk next ch-2 sp, [sc in next dc, ch 3] 7 times**, shell in ch sp of next shell, rep from * around, ending last rep at **, join in beg sc.

Rnd 4: Sl st in next dc and in ch-2 sp, beg shell in same ch sp, *ch 3, sk next ch-3 sp, [sc in next ch-3 sp, ch 3] 6 times**, shell in ch sp of next shell, rep from * around, ending last rep at **, join in 3rd ch of beg ch-3.

Rnd 5: Sl st in next dc and in ch-2 sp, beg double shell in same ch sp, *ch 3, sk next ch-3 sp, [sc in next ch-3 sp, ch 3] 5 times**, double shell in ch-2 sp of next shell, rep from * around, ending last rep at **, join in top of beg sc. Fasten off.

First Border Pineapple

Row 6: Join with sl st in first unworked ch-2 sp of rnd 5 to the right of next Pineapple, beg shell in same ch sp, ch 3, sk next ch-3 sp, [sc in next ch-3 sp, ch 3] 4 times, shell in ch sp of next shell, turn.

Rows 7–10: Rep rows 38–41 of First Pineapple of Cover.

Next Border Pineapples

Rnds 6–10: Rep Rows 6–10 of First Border Pineapple for each of 15 Border Pineapples.

Top Edging

Working in starting ch on opposite side of rnd 1 on Cover, join with sl st in any ch-2 sp, ch 3, 4 dc in same ch sp, [(sc, picot) in next ch-2 sp, 5 dc in next ch-2 sp] around, ending with (sc, picot) in last ch-2 sp, join in 3rd ch of beg ch-3. Fasten off.

Finishing

If using a cloth lampshade, cover with plastic wrap. Wet crocheted Lampshade Cover; roll in towel to squeeze out water. Fit over lamp shade, smooth and let dry.

Remove from lampshade. Weave ribbon through sts at top of crocheted piece, tie ends in bow. Sew 1 ribbon rose at top of each bottom pineapple, as shown in photo.

Remove plastic wrap from lampshade, replace with crocheted Cover. ❏❏

Pineapple Angel

Design by Jo Ann Maxwell

FINISHED SIZE
19½ inches tall to top of Wings

MATERIALS
- ❑ Size 10 crochet cotton: 400 yds natural
- ❑ Size 5/1.90mm steel crochet hook or size needed to obtain gauge
- ❑ Stringlets doll hair by All Cooped Up
- ❑ 2 inch white dove
- ❑ 1-inch pink satin roses with leaves: 10
- ❑ 2 yds ½-inch-wide gold ribbon
- ❑ 2⅔ yds ⅛-inch-wide green satin ribbon
- ❑ 4⅓ yds ¼-inch-wide green satin ribbon
- ❑ 6mm pearl beads: 10
- ❑ 1 yd strung pearls
- ❑ Small amount gold gypsophila
- ❑ Powdered blush
- ❑ Small piece of nylon stocking
- ❑ 20 x 30-inch piece poster board
- ❑ 12-inch-tall plastic foam cone
- ❑ Wide cellophane tape
- ❑ Large bowl
- ❑ 2 inch-diameter plastic foam ball
- ❑ 1½-inch diameter plastic foam ball
- ❑ 1½-inch plastic foam egg
- ❑ Hot-glue gun
- ❑ Fabric stiffener
- ❑ Plastic wrap
- ❑ Fiberfill
- ❑ Plastic drinking straw
- ❑ Clear spray paint

GAUGE
34 dc = 5 inches

PATTERN NOTES
Join with slip stitch as indicated unless otherwise stated.

Chain-2 at beginning of row or round counts as first half double crochet unless otherwise stated.

Chain-3 at beginning of row or round counts as first double crochet unless otherwise stated.

SPECIAL STITCHES
Beginning shell (beg shell): Ch 3, (dc, ch 2, 2 dc) in indicated st or sp.

Shell: (2 dc, ch 2, 2 dc) in indicated st or ch sp.

Picot: Ch 3, sl st in last sc.

Beginning double shell (beg double shell): (Beg shell, ch 2, 2 dc) in indicated ch sp.

Double shell: (Shell, ch 2, 2 dc) in indicated ch sp.

INSTRUCTIONS

ANGEL
Body
Rnd 1: Beg at top of head, ch 6, sl st in first ch to form ring, **ch 3** (see Pattern Notes), 31 dc in ring, **join** (see Pattern Notes) in 3rd ch of beg ch-3. (32 dc)

Rnds 2–10: **Ch 2** (see Pattern Notes), hdc in each st around, join in 2nd ch of beg ch-2. At end of rnd 10, insert 1½-inch plastic foam ball, join in 2nd ch of beg ch-2. (32 hdc)

Rnd 11: Ch 1, sc in first st, sk next st, [sc in next st, sk next st] around, join in beg sc. (16 sc)

Rnd 12: Ch 3, dc in same st, 2 dc in each st around, join in 3rd ch of beg ch-3. (32 dc)

Rnds 13–17: Ch 3, dc in each st around, join in 3rd ch of beg ch-3. (32 dc)

Rnd 18: Ch 1, sc in first st, [ch 4, sc in next dc] around, ending with ch 2, hdc in beg sc to form last ch-4 sp. (32 ch-4 sps)

Rnds 19–21: Ch 1, sc in ch sp just formed, [ch 4, sc in next ch sp] around, ending with ch 2, hdc in beg sc to form last ch sp.

Rnds 22–26: Ch 1, sc in ch sp just formed, [ch 5, sc in next ch sp] around, ending with ch 2, dc in beg sc to form last ch sp.

Rnds 27–30: Ch 1, sc in ch sp just formed, [ch 6, sc in next ch sp] around, ending with ch 3, dc in beg sc to form last ch sp.

Rnds 31–34: Ch 1, sc in ch sp just formed, [ch 7, sc in next ch sp] around, ending with ch 3, tr in beg sc to form last sp.

Rnd 35: Sl st in ch sp just formed, **beg shell** (see Special Stitches) in same ch sp, *ch 3, sc in next ch sp, ch 3**, **shell** (see Special Stitches) in next ch sp, rep from * around, ending last rep at **, join in 3rd ch of beg ch-3. (16 shells)

Rnd 36: Sl st in next dc and in ch-2 sp, beg shell in same ch sp, *ch 3, (dc, ch 2) in each of first 2 dc of next shell, (dc, ch 2) 4 times in ch-2 sp of same shell, dc in next dc of same shell, ch 2, dc in last dc of same shell, ch 3**, shell in ch sp of next shell, rep from * around, ending last rep at **, join in 3rd ch of beg ch-3. (8 shells)

Rnd 37: Sl st in next dc and in ch-2 sp, beg shell in same ch sp, *ch 3, sk next ch-3 sp, [sc in next dc, ch 3] 8 times**, shell in ch sp of next shell, rep from * around, ending last rep at **, join in 3rd ch of beg ch-3.

Rnd 38: Sl st in next dc and in ch-2 sp, beg shell in same ch sp, *ch 3, sk next ch-3 sp, [sc in next ch-3 sp, ch 3] 7 times**, shell in ch sp of next shell, rep from * around, ending last rep at **, join in 3rd ch of beg ch-3.

Rnd 39: Sl st in next dc and in ch-2 sp, **beg double shell** (see Special Stitches) in same ch sp, *ch 3, sk next ch-3 sp, [sc in next ch-3 sp, ch 3] 6 times**, **double shell** (see Special Stitches) in ch sp of next shell, rep from * around, ending last rep at **, join in 3rd ch of beg ch-3.

Rnd 40: Sl st in next dc and in ch-2 sp, beg shell in same ch sp, shell in next ch-2 sp, *ch 3, sk next ch-3 sp, [sc in next ch-3 sp, ch 3] 5 times**, [shell in next ch-2 sp] twice, rep from * around, ending last rep at **, join in 3rd ch of beg ch-3. Fasten off.

First Pineapple

Row 41: Join in ch sp of first unworked shell on rnd 40 to the right of next Pineapple, beg shell in same ch sp, ch 3, sk next ch-3 sp, [sc in next ch-3 sp, ch 3] 4 times, shell in ch sp of next shell, leaving rem sts unworked, turn.

Row 42: Ch 3, shell in ch sp of first shell, ch 3, sk next ch-3 sp, [sc in next ch-3 sp, ch 3] 3 times, shell in ch sp of next shell, turn.

Row 43: Ch 3, shell in ch sp of first shell, ch 3, sk next ch-3 sp, [sc in next ch-3 sp, ch 3] twice, shell in ch sp of next shell, turn.

Row 44: Ch 3, shell in ch sp of first shell, ch 3, sk next ch-3 sp, sc in next ch-3 sp, ch 3, shell in ch sp of next shell, turn.

Row 45: Ch 3, shell in ch sp of each of next 2 shells, ch 3, sl st in first dc of first shell of last row. Fasten off.

Next Pineapples

Rep rows 41–45 for each of rem 7 Pineapples.

Wing
Make 2.

Row 1: Ch 4, sl st in first ch to form ring, **ch 3** (see Pattern Notes), 6 dc in ring, turn. (7 dc)

Row 2: Ch 6 (counts as first dc and ch-3), dc in next dc, [ch 3, dc in next dc] 5 times, turn.

Row 3: Ch 7 (counts as first dc and ch-4), [dc in next dc, ch 4] 5 times, sk next 3 chs, dc in next ch, turn.

Row 4: Beg shell in first dc, [shell in next dc] 5 times, sk next 4 chs, shell in next ch, turn. (7 shells)

Row 5: Ch 3, shell in ch sp of first shell, [ch 1, shell in ch sp of next shell] twice, ch 1, dc in ch sp of next shell, (ch 1, dc) 7 times in same ch sp, [ch 1, shell in ch sp of next shell] 3 times, turn.

Row 6: Ch 3, shell in ch sp of next shell, ch 1, dc in ch sp of next shell, (ch 1, dc) 5 times in same ch sp, ch 1, shell in ch sp of next shell, ch 3, sk next ch-1 sp, [sc in next dc, ch 3] 8 times, shell in ch sp of next shell, ch 1, dc in ch sp of next shell, (ch 1, dc) 9 times in same ch sp, ch 1, shell in ch sp of next shell, turn.

Row 7: Ch 3, shell in ch sp of first shell, ch 3, sk ch-1 sp, [sc in next dc, ch 3] 10 times, shell in ch sp of next shell, ch 3, sk next ch-3 sp, [sc in next ch-3 sp, ch 3] 7 times, shell in ch sp of next shell, ch 3, sk ch-1 sp, [sc in next dc, ch 3] 6 times, shell in ch sp of next shell, turn.

Row 8: Ch 3, shell in ch sp of first shell, ch 3, sk next ch-3 sp, [sc in next ch-3 sp, ch 3] 5 times, shell in ch sp of next shell, ch 3, sk next ch-3 sp, [sc in next ch-3 sp, ch 3] 6 times, shell in ch sp of next shell, ch 3, sk next ch-3 sp, [sc in next ch-3 sp, ch 3] 9 times, shell in ch sp of next shell, turn.

Row 9: Ch 3, shell in ch sp of first shell, ch 3, sk next ch-3 sp, [sc in next ch-3 sp, ch 3] 8 times, double shell in ch sp of next shell, ch 3, sk next ch-3 sp, [sc in next ch-3 sp, ch 3] 5 times, double shell in ch sp of next shell, ch 3, sk next ch-3 sp, [sc in next ch-3 sp, ch 3] 4 times, shell in ch sp of next shell, turn.

Bottom Pineapple

Rows 10–13: Rep rows 42–45 of Body.

Center Pineapple

Row 10: Join in next unworked ch-2 sp of row 9, beg shell in same ch sp, ch 3, sk next ch-3 sp, [sc in next ch-3 sp, ch 3] 4 times, shell in next ch-2 sp, turn.

Rows 11–14: Rep rows 42–45 of Body.

Top Pineapple

Row 10: Join in next unworked ch-2 sp of row 9, beg shell in same ch sp, ch 3, sk next ch-3 sp, [sc in next ch-3 sp, ch 3] 7 times, shell in ch sp of next shell, turn.

Row 11: Ch 3, shell in ch sp of first shell, ch 3, sk next ch-3 sp, [sc in next ch-3 sp, ch 3] 6 times, shell in ch sp of next shell, turn.

Row 12: Ch 3, shell in ch sp of first shell, ch 3, sk next ch-3 sp, [sc in next ch-3 sp, ch 3] 5 times, shell in ch sp of next shell, turn.

Row 13: Ch 3, shell in ch sp of first shell, ch 3, sk next ch-3 sp, [sc in next ch-3 sp, ch 3] 4 times, shell in ch sp of next shell, turn.

Rows 14–17: Rep rows 42–45 of Body.

Sleeve
Make 2.

Rnd 1: Ch 4, sl st in first ch to form ring, ch 1, sc in ring, [ch 4, sc in ring] 7 times, ch 2, hdc in beg sc to form last ch-4 sp. (8 ch-4 sps)

Rnds 2–6: Ch 1, sc in ch sp just formed, [ch 4, sc in next ch sp] around, ending with ch 2, hdc in beg sc to form last ch sp. At end of rnd 5, cover small piece of fiberfill with plastic wrap, insert in Sleeve. (8 ch-4 sps)

Rnd 7: Ch 1, sc in this ch sp and in each ch sp around, join in beg sc. (8 sc)

Rnds 8–13: Ch 3, dc in each st around, join in 3rd ch of beg ch-3. At end of last rnd, fasten off. (8 dc)

Shaping

Cut poster board to make 12-inch-tall cone with 9 inch-diameter opening at bottom and 2 inch-diameter opening at top, tape tog with wide cellophane tape.

Place plastic foam cone inside paper cone, trimming as necessary to fit, tape to inverted bowl.

Cut 2 inch-diameter plastic foam ball in half, place flat side down on top of cone. Cover all with plastic wrap.

Apply fabric stiffener to Angel, squeeze out excess. Cover plastic foam egg with small piece of nylon stocking, then with plastic wrap, place in bodice, wide end first. Trim excess plastic wrap and panty hose, leaving enough to grasp with pliers when removing egg later.

Place Angel over cone, wrapping a strand of crochet cotton tightly around rnd 11 of Body to shape neck, and less tightly between rnds 16 and 17 of Body to shape waist. Let dry.

Cut crochet cotton from waist only, remove egg with pliers, twisting foam to pull out.

Apply fabric stiffener to Wings, pin tog to dry with piece of plastic wrap between so Wings will be same shape.

Cut drinking straw in half, place 1 piece in bottom of each Sleeve. Apply fabric stiffener to Sleeves, let dry.

Remove straws. Remove fiberfill and plastic wrap with a crochet hook through ch-4 sps of upper Sleeve.

Finishing

Lightly spray all pieces with clear spray paint, let dry.

Wrap length of ¼ inch-wide ribbon twice around bodice, crossing at front as shown in photo, glue ends tog in back.

Bend Wings at center, glue to back of Angel with largest pineapple at top. Using photo as a guide, glue Sleeves to sides of Body.

Weave rem ¼-inch wide green and gold ribbons through sps around bottom of skirt above pineapples. Decorate as shown in photo using gold gypsophila, 7 roses and 6mm pearls.

Cut doll hair approximately 5 inches long, glue to head. Loosely wrap small length of strung pearls twice across top of head for halo; glue to secure. Glue small sprig of gold gypsophila to hair.

Cut 2 pieces of ⅛-inch-wide ribbon each 24 inches long. Holding both tog, tie a bow, glue to outside of Sleeve at rnd 7, trimming ends as desired.

Rep for opposite Sleeve.

Glue dove between bottoms of Sleeves, adding green ribbon, strings of pearls, gold gypsophila and 3 rem satin roses as shown in photo.

Lightly apply small amount of blush to cheeks. ❑❑

Pineapple Afghan

Design by Jo Ann Maxwell

SKILL LEVEL

INTERMEDIATE

FINISHED SIZE

54 x 72 inches

MATERIALS

- ❑ Red Heart Super Saver Jumbo size medium (worsted) weight yarn (16 oz/835 yds/453g per skein):
  3 skeins #0316 soft white
- ❑ Size J/10/6mm crochet hook or size needed to obtain gauge

GAUGE

Rnds 1–5 on Motif = 4½ inches

PATTERN NOTES

Join with a slip stitch as indicated unless otherwise stated.

Chain-3 at beginning of row or round counts as first double crochet unless otherwise stated.

SPECIAL STITCHES

Beginning shell (beg shell): Ch 3 *(see Pattern Notes)*, (dc, ch 2, 2 dc) in place indicated.

Shell: (2 dc, ch 2, 2 dc) in place indicated.

INSTRUCTIONS

AFGHAN

First Motif

Rnd 1: Ch 4, sl st in first ch to form ring, ch 1, 9 sc in ring, **join** *(see Pattern Notes)* in beg sc. *(9 sc)*

Rnd 2: Ch 1, sc in first st, ch 2, [sc in next sc, ch 2] around, join in beg sc. *(9 ch-2 sps)*

Rnd 3: Ch 1, (sc, 4 dc, sc) in each ch-2 sp around, join in beg sc of rnd 2. *(9 petals)*

Rnd 4: Ch 1, sc in first st, ch 3, [working from behind rnd 3 petals, sc in next sc on rnd 2, ch 3] around, join in beg sc of rnd 4. *(9 ch-3 sps)*

Rnd 5: Ch 1, (sc, 5 dc, sc) in each ch-3 sp around, join in beg sc of rnd 4. *(9 petals)*

Rnd 6: Ch 1, sc in first st, ch 5, [working behind rnd 5 petals, sc in next sc on rnd 4, ch 5] around, join in beg sc of rnd 6. *(9 ch-5 sps)*

Rnd 7: Sl st in next ch-5 sp, **ch 3** *(see Pattern Notes)*, (2 dc, ch 2, 3 dc) in same ch sp, (3 dc, ch 2, 3 dc) in each ch-5 sp around, join in 3rd ch of beg ch-3.

Rnd 8: Sl st back in sp between last dc just made and beg ch-3 of rnd 7, ch 1, sc in same ch sp, *ch 5, sc in next ch-2 sp, ch 5**, sk next 3 dc, sc in sp before next dc, rep from * around, ending last rep at **, join in beg sc. *(18 ch-5 sps)*

Rnd 9: Sl st in each of next 3 chs, ch 1, sc in same ch sp, ch 6, [sc in next ch-5 sp, ch 6] around, join in beg sc. Fasten off. *(18 ch-6 sps)*

Remaining Motifs

Make 23.

Rnds 1–8: Rep rnds 1–8 of First Motif.

Rnd 9 (joining): Sl st in each of next 3 chs, ch 1, sc in same ch sp,

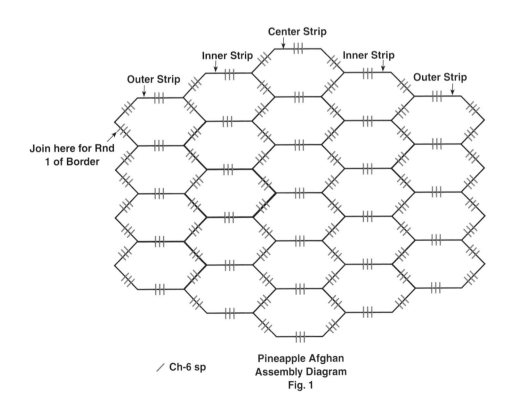

/ Ch-6 sp

**Pineapple Afghan
Assembly Diagram
Fig. 1**

ch 3, sl st in ch-6 sp on previous Motif, ch 3, sc in next ch-5 sp on working Motif, [ch 3, sl st in next ch-6 sp on previous Motif, ch 3, sc in next ch-5 sp on working Motif] twice (3 ch-6 sps; 1 adjacent side joined), complete rnd as for First Motif. Fasten off.

Assembly

Make and join a total of 6 Motifs for center strip, leaving 6 ch-6 sps free on each side of joined section according to diagram (see Fig. 1, page 10).

Make and join 5 Motifs on each side of center strip for inner strips, joining as many adjacent sides as necessary in same manner as for 2nd Motif.

Make and join 4 Motifs to each outside edge of each inner strip for outer strips. There will be 102 unworked ch-6 sps around outside edge when last Motif is joined.

Pineapple Border

Rnd 1: With RS facing, join with sl st in ch-6 sp indicated in Fig. 1, ch 1, sc in same ch sp, working in unworked ch-6 sps around, *[ch 6, sc in next ch-6 sp] 17 times, ch 3, [**shell** (see Special Stitches) in next ch-6 sp, ch 2] twice, shell in next ch-6 sp, ch 3, **sc in next ch-6 sp, [ch 6, sc in next ch-6 sp] 11 times, ch 3, [shell in next ch-6 sp, ch 2] twice, shell in next ch-6 sp, ch 3**, rep between **, sc in next ch-6 sp, rep from * around, join in beg sc.

Rnd 2: Sl st in each of next 3 chs, ch 1, sc in same sp, work the following steps to complete rnd:

  A. ◊*Ch 3, [shell in next ch-6 sp, ch 2] twice, shell in next ch-6 sp, ch 3, sc in next ch-6 sp, [ch 6, sc in next ch-6 sp] twice*, rep between * once;

  B. Ch 3, [shell in next ch-6 sp, ch 2] twice, shell in next ch-6 sp, ch 3, sc in next ch-6 sp;

  C. Ch 6, shell in ch sp of next shell, ch 3, sc in next ch-2 sp, dc in next shell sp, (ch 1, dc) 7 times in same sp, sc in next ch-2 sp, ch 3, shell in ch sp of next shell, ch 6, sc in next ch-6 sp;

  D. [Rep between * of step A once, rep step B once, rep step C] twice, rep from ◊ around, join in beg sc.

Rnd 3: Sl st in each of next 3 chs, in next 2 dc and in next ch-2 sp, beg shell in ch sp, ◊*ch 3, sc in next ch-2 sp, dc in ch sp of next shell, (ch 1, dc) 6 times in same ch sp, sc in next ch-2 sp, ch 3, shell in ch sp of next shell, ch 3, sc in next ch-6 sp, ch 6, sc in next ch-6 sp, ch 3, shell in next shell sp*, rep between *, ch 3, sc in next ch-2 sp, dc in ch sp of next shell, (ch 1, dc) 6 times in same ch sp, sc in next ch-2 sp, ch 3, shell in ch sp of next shell, ch 3, sc in next ch-6 sp, ch 6, ***shell in ch sp of next shell, ch 3, sk next ch-3 sp, [sc in next dc, ch 3] 8 times, shell in ch sp of next shell, ch 6, sc in next ch-6 sp, ch 3, shell in ch sp of next shell***, [rep between * once, ch 3, sc in next ch-2 sp, dc in ch sp of next shell, (ch 1, dc) 6 times in same ch sp, sc in next ch-2 sp, ch 3, shell in ch sp of next shell, ch 3, sc in next ch-6 sp, ch 6, rep between *** once] twice, rep from ◊ around, join in 3rd ch of beg ch-3.

Rnd 4: Sl st in next dc and in ch-2 sp, beg shell in same sp, ◊*ch 3, sk next ch-3 sp, [sc in next dc, ch 3] 7 times, shell in ch sp of next shell, ch 6, sc in next ch-6 sp, ch 6, shell in ch sp of next shell*, **rep between * twice, ch 3, sk next ch-3 sp, [sc in next ch-3 sp, ch 3] 7 times, shell in ch sp of next shell, ch 6, sc in next ch-6 sp, ch 6, shell in ch sp of next shell, rep from ** twice, rep from ◊ around, join in 3rd ch of beg ch-3.

Rnd 5: Sl st in next dc and in ch-2 sp, **beg shell** (see Special Stitches) in same ch sp, *ch 3, sk next ch-3 sp, [sc in next ch-3 sp, ch 3] 6 times, shell in ch sp of next shell, ch 3, sc in next ch-6 sp, ch 6, sc in next ch-6 sp, ch 3, shell in ch sp of next shell, rep from * around, join in 3rd ch of beg ch-3.

First Pineapple

Row 6: Now working in rows, sl st in next dc and in ch-2 sp, beg shell in same ch sp, ch 3, sk next ch-3 sp, [sc in next ch-3 sp, ch 3] 5 times, shell in ch sp of next shell, leaving rem sts unworked, turn.

Row 7: Ch 3, shell in ch sp of first shell, ch 3, sk next ch-3 sp, [sc in next ch-3 sp, ch 3] 4 times, shell in ch sp of next shell, turn.

Row 8: Ch 3, shell in ch sp of first shell, ch 3, sk next ch-3 sp, [sc in next ch-3 sp, ch 3] 3 times, shell in ch sp of next shell, turn.

Row 9: Ch 3, shell in ch sp of first shell, ch 3, sk next ch-3 sp, [sc in next ch-3 sp, ch 3] twice, shell in ch sp of next shell, turn.

Row 10: Ch 3, shell in ch sp of first shell, ch 3, sk next ch-3 sp, sc in next ch-3 sp, ch 3, shell in ch sp of next shell, turn.

Row 11: Ch 3, shell in ch sp of each of next 2 shells. Fasten off.

2nd Pineapple

Row 6: With RS facing, join with sl st in ch sp of next unworked shell on rnd 5, beg shell in same ch sp, ch 3, sk next ch-3 sp, [sc in next ch-3 sp, ch 3] 5 times, shell in ch sp of next shell, turn.

Rows 7–11: Rep rows 7–11 of First Pineapple. At end of last Pineapple, **do not fasten off**, turn.

Rnd 12: Now working in rnds, ch 1, sc in last dc made, *[ch 4, sc in ch sp of next shell] twice, working in ends of rows, [ch 4, sc in end of next row, ch 4, sc in end of next row] 3 times, ch 4, sc in next ch-6 sp, beg with next row 6, [ch 4, sc in end of next row] 6 times to top of Pineapple, rep from * around, ending with [ch 4, sc in end of next row] 5 times, ch 4, join in beg sc.

Rnd 13: Sl st in each of next 2 chs, ch 1, sc in same ch sp, ◊*dc in next ch-4 sp, (ch 1, dc) 6 times in same ch sp, sc in next ch-4 sp*, [dc in next ch-4 sp, (ch 1, dc) 4 times in same ch sp, sc in next ch sp] 4 times, sc in next ch-4 sp, rep between * once, rep from ◊ around, join in beg sc. Fasten off.

Remaining Pineapples

Rep rows 6–13 of 2nd Pineapple for each of rem 18 Pineapples.

Finishing

Wash Afghan, spin-dry. Spread Afghan on towels on flat surface.

Shape each flower, iron lightly over each flower using damp pressing cloth for approximately 2 seconds, shape petals again. Let dry. ❑❑

Round Tablecloth

Design by Jo Ann Maxwell

SKILL LEVEL

INTERMEDIATE

FINISHED SIZE
43 inches in diameter

MATERIALS
- ❑ Size 10 crochet:
  1,400 yds natural
- ❑ Size 5/1.90mm steel crochet hook or size needed to obtain gauge

GAUGE
Rnds 1–3 = 2½ inches in diameter

PATTERN NOTES
Join with slip stitch as indicated unless otherwise stated.

Chain-3 at beginning of row or round counts as first double crochet unless otherwise stated.

SPECIAL STITCHES
Beginning shell (beg shell): Ch 3, (dc, ch 2, 2 dc) in place indicated.

Shell: (2 dc, ch 2, 2 dc) in place indicated.

Picot: Ch 3, sl st in last sc.

Beginning double shell (beg double shell): (Beg shell, ch 2, 2 dc) in place indicated.

Double shell: (Shell, ch 2, 2 dc) in place indicated

INSTRUCTIONS
TABLECLOTH
Rnd 1: Ch 4, sl st in first ch to form ring, **ch 3** *(see Pattern Notes)*, 19 dc in ring, **join** *(see Pattern Notes)* in 3rd ch of beg ch-3. *(20 dc)*

Rnd 2: Ch 4 *(counts as first tr)*, tr in same st, ch 3, [sk next st, 2 tr in next st, ch 3] around, join in 4th ch of beg ch-4.

Rnd 3: Ch 3, dc in same st, ch 2, 2 dc in next tr, *ch 1, sc in next ch sp, ch 1**, 2 dc in next tr, ch 2, 2 dc in next tr, rep from * around, ending last rep at **, join in 3rd ch of beg ch-3.

Rnd 4: Sl st in next dc and in ch-2 sp, **beg shell** *(see Special Stitches)*

in same ch sp, ch 5, [**shell** *(see Special Stitches)* in next ch-2 sp, ch 5] around, join in 3rd ch of beg ch-3. *(10 shells)*

Rnd 5: Sl st in next dc and in ch-2 sp, beg shell in same sp, *ch 3, sc in next ch-5 sp, ch 3**, shell in ch sp of next shell, rep from * around, ending last rep at **, join in 3rd ch of beg ch-3.

Rnd 6: Sl st in next dc and in ch-2 sp, ch 3, 8 dc in same ch sp, *sc in next ch-3 sp, ch 5, sc in next ch-3 sp**, 9 dc in ch sp of next shell, rep from

* around, ending last rep at **, join in 3rd ch of beg ch-3.

Rnd 7: Sl st in each of next 4 dc, ch 10 *(counts as first dc and ch-7)*, *(sc, **picot**—*see Special Stitches*) in next ch-5 sp, ch 7**, dc in 5th dc of next 9-dc group, ch 7, rep from * around, ending last rep at **, join in 3rd ch of beg ch-10.

Rnd 8: Beg shell in same st as joining, *ch 2, sc in next ch-7 sp, ch-7, sc in next ch-7 sp, ch 2**, shell in next dc, rep from * around, ending last rep at **, join in 3rd ch of beg ch-3.

Rnd 9: Sl st in next dc and in ch-2 sp, beg shell in same ch sp, *ch 5, shell in 4th ch of next ch-7, ch 5**, shell in ch sp of next shell, rep from * around, ending last rep at **, join in 3rd ch of beg ch-3.

Rnd 10: Sl st in next dc and in ch-2 sp, beg shell in same ch sp, *ch 2, sc in next ch-5 sp, dc in ch sp of next shell, (ch 1, dc) 7 times in same ch sp, sc in next ch-5 sp, ch 2**, shell in ch sp of next shell, rep from * around, ending last rep at **, join in 3rd ch of beg ch-3.

Rnd 11: Sl st in next dc and in ch-2 sp, **beg double shell** (see Special Stitches) in same ch sp, *ch 3, sk next ch-2 sp, [sc in next dc, ch 3] 8 times**, **double shell** (see Special Stitches) in ch sp of next shell, rep from * around, ending last rep at **, join in 3rd ch of beg ch-3.

Rnd 12: Sl st in next dc and in ch-2 sp, beg shell in same ch sp, *ch 1, shell in next ch-2 sp, ch 3, sk next ch-3 sp, [sc in next ch-3 sp, ch 3] 7 times**, shell in next ch-2 sp, rep from * around, ending last rep at **, join in 3rd ch of beg ch-3.

Rnd 13: Sl st in next dc and in ch-2 sp, beg shell in same sp, *ch 2, shell in ch sp of next shell, ch 3, sk next ch-3 sp, [sc in next ch-3 sp, ch 3] 6 times**, shell in ch sp of next shell, rep from * around, ending last rep at **, join in 3rd ch of beg ch-3.

Rnd 14: Sl st in next dc and in ch-2 sp, beg shell in same ch sp, *ch 3, shell in ch sp of next shell, ch 3, sk next ch-3 sp, [sc in next ch-3 sp, ch 3] 5 times**, shell in ch sp of next shell, rep from * around, ending last rep at **, join in 3rd ch of beg ch-3.

Rnd 15: Sl st in next dc and in ch-2 sp, beg shell in same ch sp, *ch 3, sc in next ch-3 sp, ch 3, shell in ch sp of next shell, ch 3, sk next ch-3 sp, [sc in next ch-3 sp, ch 3] 4 times**, shell in ch sp of next shell, rep from * around, ending last rep at **, join in 3rd ch of beg ch-3.

Rnd 16: Sl st in next dc and in ch-2 sp, beg shell in same ch sp, *ch 3, sc in next ch-3 sp, ch 5, sc in next ch-3 sp, ch 3, shell in ch sp of next shell, ch 3, sk next ch-3 sp, [sc in next ch-3 sp, ch 3] 3 times**, shell in ch sp of next shell, rep from * around, ending last rep at **, join in 3rd ch of beg ch-3.

Rnd 17: Sl st in next dc and in ch-2 sp, beg shell in same ch sp, *ch 3, sc in next ch-3 sp, ch 5, sk first ch of next ch-5 sp, dc in each of next 3 chs, ch 5, sc in next ch-3 sp, ch 3, shell in ch sp of next shell, ch 3, sk next ch-3 sp, [sc in next ch-3 sp, ch 3] twice**, shell in ch sp of next shell, rep from * around, ending last rep at **, join in 3rd ch of beg ch-3.

Rnd 18: Sl st in next dc and in ch-2 sp, beg shell in same ch sp, *sc in next ch-3 sp, ch 5, dc in each of last 3 chs of next ch-5 sp, ch 5, sk 3 dc, dc in each of first 3 chs of next ch-5 sp, ch 5, sc in next ch-3 sp, ch 3, shell in ch sp of next shell, ch 3, sk next ch-3 sp, sc in next ch-3 sp, ch 3**, shell in ch sp of next shell, rep from * around, ending last rep at **, join in 3rd ch of beg ch-3.

Rnd 19: Sl st in next dc and in ch-2 sp, beg shell in same ch sp, *ch 3, sc in next ch-3 sp, ch 5, dc in each of last 3 chs of next ch-5 sp, ch 5, sc in next ch-5 sp, ch 5, sk next 3 dc, dc in each of first 3 chs of next ch-5 sp, ch 5, sc in next ch-3 sp, ch 3**, [shell in ch sp of next shell] twice, rep from * around, ending last rep at **, shell in ch sp of next shell, join in 3rd ch of beg ch-3.

Rnd 20: Sl st in next dc and in ch-2 sp, ch 1, sc in same ch sp, *ch 5, sc in next ch-3 sp, ch 5, dc in each of last 3 chs of next ch-5 sp, ch 5, sc in 5th ch of next ch-5 sp, sc in next sc, sc in first ch of next ch-5 sp, ch 5, sk next 3 dc, dc in each of first 3 chs of next ch-5 sp, ch 5, sc in next ch-3 sp**, [ch 5, sc in ch sp of next shell] twice, rep from * around, ending last rep at **, ch 5, sc in ch sp of next shell, ch 5, join in beg sc.

Rnd 21: Sl st in each of next 3 chs, ch 1, sc in same ch sp, *ch 5, dc in each of last 3 chs of next ch-5 sp, ch 5, sc in last ch of next ch-5 sp, sc in each of next 3 sc, sc in first ch of next ch-5 sp, ch 5, sk next 3 dc, dc in each of first 3 chs of next ch-5 sp, ch 5, sc in next ch-5 sp, ch 5, (sc, ch 5) 4 times in next ch-5 sp**, sc in next ch-5 sp, rep from * around, ending last rep at **, join in beg sc.

Rnd 22: Sl st in each of next 3 chs, ch 1, sc in same ch sp, *ch 5, dc in each of first 3 chs of next ch-5 sp, ch 5, sk next sc, sc in each of next 3 sc, ch 5, dc in each of last 3 chs of next ch-5 sp, ch 5, [sc in next ch-5 sp, ch 5] 6 times**, sc in next ch-5 sp, rep from * around, ending last rep at **, join in beg sc.

Rnd 23: Sl st in each of next 3 chs, ch 1, sc in same ch sp, *ch 5, dc in each of first 3 chs of next ch-5 sp, ch 5, sk next sc, sc in next sc, ch 5, dc in each of last 3 chs of next ch-5 sp, ch 5, [sc in next ch-5 sp, ch 5] 7 times**, sc in next ch-5 sp, rep from * around, ending last rep at **, join in beg sc.

Rnd 24: Sl st in each of next 3 chs, ch 1, sc in same ch sp, *ch 5, dc in each of first 3 chs of next ch-5 sp, ch 3, dc in each of last 3 chs of next ch-5 sp, ch 5, [sc in next ch-5 sp, ch 5] 8 times**, sc in next ch-5 sp, rep from * around, ending last rep at **, join in beg sc.

Rnd 25: Sl st in each of next 3 chs, ch 1, sc in same ch sp, *ch 5, sk next 3 dc, dc in each of next 3 chs, ch 5, [sc in next ch-5 sp, ch 5] 9 times**, sc in next ch-5 sp, rep from * around, ending last rep at **, join in beg sc.

Rnd 26: Sl st in each of next 3 chs, ch 1, sc in same ch sp, ch 5, [sc in next ch-5 sp, ch 5] 5 times, *sk first ch of next ch-5 sp, dc in each of next 3 chs**, ch 5, [sc in next ch-5 sp, ch 5] 10 times, rep from * around, ending last rep at **, ch 5, [sc in next ch-5 sp, ch 5] 4 times, join in beg sc.

Rnd 27: Sl st in next ch-5 sp, ch 1, (sc, ch 5) 4 times in same ch sp, *[sc in next ch-5 sp, ch 5] 4 times, dc in each of last 3 chs of next ch-5 sp, ch 5, sk next 3 dc, dc in each of first 3 chs of next ch-5 sp, ch 5, [sc in next ch-5 sp, ch 5] 4 times**, (sc, ch 5) 4 times in next ch-5 sp, rep from * around, ending last rep at **, join in beg sc.

Rnd 28: Sl st in each of next 3 chs, ch 1, sc in same ch sp, ch 5, [sc in next ch-5 sp, ch 5] 6 times, *dc in each of last 3 chs of next ch-5 sp, ch 5, sc in next ch-5 sp, ch 5, dc in each of first 3 chs of next ch-5 sp, ch 5**, [sc in next ch-5 sp, ch 5] 11 times, rep from * around, ending last rep at

**, [sc in next ch-5 sp, ch 5] 4 times, join in beg sc.

Rnd 29: Sl st in each of next 3 chs, ch 1, sc in same ch sp, ch 5, [sc in next ch-5 sp, ch 5] 5 times, *dc in each of last 3 chs of next ch-5 sp, ch 5, sc in last ch of next ch-5 sp, sc in next sc, sc in next ch, ch 5, sk next 3 dc, dc in each of first 3 chs of next ch-5 sp, ch 5**, [sc in next ch-5 sp, ch 5] 10 times, rep from * around, ending last rep at **, [sc in next ch-5 sp, ch 5] 3 times, sc in next ch-5 sp, ch 2, dc in beg sc to form last ch-5 sp.

Rnd 30: Beg shell in sp just formed, *[ch 3, shell in next ch-5 sp] twice, ch 3, [sc in next ch-5 sp, ch 5] 3 times, dc in each of last 3 chs of next ch-5 sp, ch 5, sc in last ch of next ch-5 sp, sc in each of next 3 sc, sc in next ch, ch 5, sk next 3 dc, dc in each of first 3 chs of next ch-5 sp, [ch 5, sc in next ch-5 sp] 3 times, ch 3**, shell in next ch-5 sp, rep from * around, ending last rep at **, join in 3rd ch of beg ch-3.

Rnd 31: Sl st in next dc and in ch-2 sp, beg shell in same ch sp, *ch 3, sc in next ch-3 sp, 8 dc in ch sp of next shell, sc in next ch-3 sp, ch 3, shell in ch sp of next shell, ch 3, [sc in next ch-5 sp, ch 5] 3 times, sk next 3 dc, dc in each of first 3 chs of next ch-5 sp, ch 5, sk next sc, sc in each of next 3 sc, ch 5, dc in each of last 3 chs of next ch-5 sp, [ch 5, sc in next ch-5 sp] 3 times, ch 3**, shell in ch sp of next shell, rep from * around, ending last rep at **, join in 3rd ch of beg ch-3.

Rnd 32: Sl st in next dc and in ch-2 sp, beg shell in same ch sp, *ch 3, sk next ch-3 sp, [sc in next dc, ch 3] 8 times, shell in ch sp of next shell, ch 3, sk next ch-3 sp, [sc in next ch-5 sp, ch 5] 3 times, sk next 3 dc, dc in each of first 3 chs of next ch-5 sp, ch 5, sk next sc, sc in next sc, ch 5, dc in each of last 3 chs of next ch-5 sp, [ch 5, sc in next ch-5 sp] 3 times, ch 3**, shell in ch sp of next shell, rep from * around, ending last rep at **, join in 3rd ch of beg ch-3.

Rnd 33: Sl st in next dc and in ch-2 sp, beg shell in same ch sp, *ch 3, sk next ch-3 sp, [sc in next ch-3 sp, ch 3] 7 times, shell in ch sp of next shell, ch 5, sk next ch-3 sp, [sc in next ch-5 sp, ch 5] 3 times, sk next 3 dc, dc in each of first 3 chs of next ch-5 sp, ch 3, dc in each of last 3 chs of next ch-5 sp, ch 5, [sc in next ch-5 sp, ch 5] 3 times**, shell in ch sp of next shell, rep from * around, ending last rep at **, join in 3rd ch of beg ch-3.

Rnd 34: Sl st in next dc and in ch-2 sp, beg shell in same sp, *ch 3, sk next ch-3 sp, [sc in next ch-3 sp, ch 3] 6 times, shell in ch sp of next shell, ch 5, [sc in next ch-5 sp, ch 5] 4 times, sk next 3 dc, dc in each of next 3 chs, ch 5, [sc in next ch-5 sp, ch 5] 4 times**, shell in ch sp of next shell, rep from * around, ending last rep at **, join in 3rd ch of beg ch-3.

Rnd 35: Sl st in next dc and in ch-2 sp, beg shell in same ch sp, *ch 3, sk next ch-3 sp, [sc in next ch-3 sp, ch 3] 5 times, shell in ch sp of next shell, ch 5, [sc in next ch-5 sp, ch 5] 10 times**, shell in ch sp of next shell, rep from * around, ending last rep at **, join in 3rd ch of beg ch-3.

Rnd 36: Sl st in next dc and in ch-2 sp, beg shell in same ch sp, *ch 3, sk next ch-3 sp, [sc in next ch-3 sp, ch 3] 4 times, shell in ch sp of next shell, ch 5, [sc in next ch-5 sp, ch 5] 5 times, (sc, ch 5) 3 times in next ch-5 sp, [sc in next ch-5 sp, ch 5] 5 times**, shell in ch sp of next shell, rep from * around, ending last rep at **, join in 3rd ch of beg ch-3.

Rnd 37: Sl st in next dc and in ch-2 sp, beg shell in same ch sp, *ch 3, sk next ch-3 sp, [sc in next ch-3 sp, ch 3] 3 times, shell in ch sp of next shell, ch 5, [sc in next ch-5 sp, ch 5] 14 times**, shell in ch sp of next shell, rep from * around, ending last rep at **, join in 3rd ch of beg ch-3.

Rnd 38: Sl st in next dc and in ch-2 sp, beg shell in same ch sp, *ch 3, sk next ch-3 sp, [sc in next ch-3 sp, ch 3] twice, shell in ch sp of next shell, ch 5, [sc in next ch-5 sp, ch 5] 15 times**, shell in ch sp of next shell, rep from * around, ending last rep at **, join in 3rd ch of beg ch-3.

Rnd 39: Sl st in next dc and in ch-2 sp, beg shell in same ch sp, *ch 3, sk next ch-3 sp, sc in next ch-3 sp, ch 3, shell in ch sp of next shell, ch 5, [sc in next ch-5 sp, ch 5] 16 times**,

shell in ch sp of next shell, rep from * around, ending last rep at **, join in 3rd ch of beg ch-3.

Rnd 40: Sl st in next dc and in ch-2 sp, beg shell in same ch sp, shell in ch sp of next shell, *ch 5, [sc in next ch-5 sp, ch 5] 17 times **, [shell in ch sp of next shell] twice, rep from * around, ending last rep at **, join in 3rd ch of beg ch-3.

Rnd 41: Sl st in next dc and in ch-2 sp, ch 1, sc in same ch sp, ch 5, sc in ch sp of next shell, ch 5, *[sc in next ch-5 sp, ch 5] 18 times**, [sc in ch sp of next shell, ch 5] twice, rep from * around, ending last rep at **, join in beg sc.

Rnds 42 & 43: Sl st in each of next 3 chs, ch 1, sc in same sp, ch 5, [sc in next ch-5 sp, ch 5] rep around, join in beg sc.

Rnd 44: Sl st in each of next 3 chs, ch 1, sc in same ch sp, *[ch 5, sc in next ch-5 sp] 8 times, ch 3, double shell in next ch-5 sp, ch 3**, sc in next ch-5 sp, rep from * around, ending last rep at **, join in beg sc.

Rnd 45: Sl st in each of next 3 chs, ch 1, sc in same sp, *[ch 5, sc in next ch-5 sp] 7 times, [ch 3, shell in next ch-2 sp] twice, ch 3**, sc in next ch-5 sp, rep from * around, ending last rep at **, join in beg sc.

Rnd 46: Sl st in each of next 3 chs, ch 1, sc in same ch sp, *[ch 5, sc in next ch-5 sp] 6 times, ch 3, shell in ch sp of next shell, ch 3, (sc, picot) in next ch-3 sp, ch 3, shell in ch sp of next shell, ch 3**, sc in next ch-5 sp, rep from * around, ending last rep at **, join in beg sc.

Rnd 47: Sl st in each of next 3 chs, ch 1, sc in same ch sp, *[ch 5, sc in next ch-5 sp] 5 times, ch 3, shell in ch sp of next shell, ch 3, sc in next ch-3 sp, ch 5, sc in next ch-3 sp, ch 3, shell in ch sp of next shell, ch 3**, sc in next ch-5 sp, rep from* around, ending last rep at **, join in beg sc.

Rnd 48: Sl st in each of next 3 chs, ch 1, sc in same ch sp, *[ch 5, sc in next ch-5 sp] 4 times, ch 3, shell in ch sp of next shell, ch 3, sk ch-3 sp, 14 dc in next ch-5 sp, ch 3, shell in ch sp of next shell, ch 3**, sc in next ch-5 sp, rep from * around, ending last rep at **, join in beg sc.

Rnd 49: Sl st in each of next 3 chs, ch 1, sc in same ch sp, *[ch 5, sc in next ch-5 sp] 3 times, ch 3, shell in ch sp of next shell, ch 3, sc in next ch-3 sp, dc in next dc, [ch 1, dc in next dc] 13 times, sc in next ch-3 sp, ch 3, shell in ch sp of next shell, ch 3**, sc in next ch-5 sp, rep from * around, ending last rep at **, join in beg sc.

Rnd 50: Sl st in each of next 3 chs, ch 1, sc in same ch sp, *[ch 5, sc in next ch-5 sp] twice, ch 3, double shell in ch sp of next shell, ch 3, sk next ch-3 sp, [sc in next dc, ch 3] 14 times, double shell in ch sp of next shell, ch 3**, sc in next ch-5 sp, rep from * around, ending last rep at **, join in beg sc.

Rnd 51: Sl st in each of next 3 chs, ch 1, sc in same ch sp, *ch 5, sc in next ch-5 sp, [ch 3, shell in next ch-2 sp] twice, ch 3, sk next ch-3 sp, [sc in next ch-3 sp, ch 3] 13 times, [shell in next ch-2 sp, ch 3] twice**, sc in next ch-5 sp, rep from * around, ending last rep at **, join in beg sc.

Rnd 52: Sl st in each of next 3 chs, ch 1, sc in same ch sp, *ch 3, **shell in ch sp of next shell, ch 3, sc in next ch-3 sp, ch 3, shell in ch sp of next shell, ch 3, sk next ch-3 sp **, [sc in next ch-3 sp, ch 3] 12 times, rep between **, sc in next ch-3 sp, rep from * around, join in beg sc.

Rnd 53: Sl st in each of next 3 chs, in each of next 2 dc and in next ch-2 sp, ch 1, sc in same ch sp, *ch 4, [sc in next ch-3 sp, ch 4] twice, shell in ch sp of next shell, ch 3, sk next ch-3 sp, [sc in next ch-3 sp, ch 3] 11 times, shell in ch sp of next shell, ch 4, [sc in next ch-3 sp, ch 4] twice, [sc in ch sp of next shell] twice, rep from * around, ending with sc in ch sp of last shell, join in beg sc.

Rnd 54: Sl st in each of next 2 chs, ch 4 *(counts as first dc and ch-1)*, *[sc in next ch-4 sp, ch 4] twice, shell in ch sp of next shell, ch 3, sk next ch-3 sp, [sc in next ch-3 sp, ch 3] 10 times, shell in ch sp of next shell, [ch 4, sc in next ch-4 sp] twice, ch 1, dc in next ch-4 sp, ch 3**, dc in next ch-4 sp, ch 1, rep from * around, ending last rep at **, join in 3rd ch of beg ch-4.

Rnd 55: Sl st in next ch, in next sc, and in each of next 2 chs, ch 1, sc in same ch sp, *ch 4, sc in next ch-4 sp, ch 4, shell in ch sp of next shell, ch 3, sk next ch-3 sp, [sc in next ch-3 sp, ch 3] 9 times, shell in ch sp of next shell, [ch 4, sc in next ch-4 sp] twice, ch 1 [tr, ch 3, tr] in next ch-3 sp, ch 1**, sc in next ch-4 sp, rep from * around, ending last rep at **, join in beg sc.

Rnd 56: Sc in each of next 2 chs, ch 1, sc in same ch sp, *ch 4, (sc, picot) in next ch-4 sp, ch 4, shell in ch sp of next shell, ch 3, sk next ch-3 sp, [sc in next ch-3 sp, ch 3] 8 times, shell in ch sp of next shell, ch 4, (sc, picot) in next ch-4 sp, ch 4, sc in next ch-4 sp, 7 dc in next ch-3 sp**, sc in next ch-4 sp, rep from * around, ending last rep at **, join in beg sc. Fasten off.

First Pineapple
Row 57: Join in ch sp of next unworked shell of rnd 56, beg shell in same ch sp, ch 3, sk next ch-3 sp, [sc in next ch-3 sp, ch 3] 7 times, shell in ch sp of next shell, leaving last sts unworked, turn.

Row 58: Ch 3, shell in ch sp of first shell, ch 3, sk next ch-3 sp, [sc in next ch-3 sp, ch 3] 6 times, shell in ch sp of next shell, turn.

Row 59: Ch 3, shell in ch sp of first shell, ch 3, sk next ch-3 sp, [sc in next ch-3 sp, ch 3] 5 times, shell in ch sp of next shell, turn.

Row 60: Ch 3, shell in ch sp of first shell, ch 3, sk next ch-3 sp, [sc in next ch-3 sp, ch 3] 4 times, shell in ch sp of next shell, turn.

Row 61: Ch 3, shell in ch sp of first shell, ch 3, sk next ch-3 sp, [sc in next ch-3 sp, ch 3] 3 times, shell in ch sp of next shell, turn.

Row 62: Ch 3, shell in ch sp of first shell, ch 3, sk next ch-3 sp, [sc in next ch-3 sp, ch 3] twice, shell in ch sp of next shell, turn.

Row 63: Ch 3, shell in ch sp of first shell, ch 3, sk next ch-3 sp, sc in next ch-3 sp, ch 3, shell in ch sp of next shell, turn.

Row 64: Ch 3, [shell in ch sp of next shell] twice. Fasten off.

Next Pineapples
Rows 57–64: Rep rows 57–64 for each of rem 19 Pineapples. ❏❏

Small Pineapple Doily

Design by Jo Ann Maxwell

SKILL LEVEL

INTERMEDIATE

FINISHED SIZE

14 inches in diameter

MATERIALS

- ❑ South Maid crochet cotton size 10 (350 yds per ball): 1 ball #430 cream
- ❑ Size 5/1.90mm steel crochet hook or size needed to obtain gauge

GAUGE

First 2 rnds = 1¾ inches in diameter

PATTERN NOTES

Join with slip stitch as indicated unless otherwise stated.

Chain-3 at beginning of row or round counts as first double crochet unless otherwise stated.

SPECIAL STITCHES

Chain-3 picot (ch-3 picot): Ch 3, sl st in last sc.

7-picot loop (7-picot lp): [Ch 4, sl st into 4th ch from hook] 7 times, sl st in last sc.

Beginning shell (beg shell): Ch 3 (see Pattern Notes), (dc, ch 2, 2 dc) in place indicated.

Shell: (2 dc, ch 2, 2 dc) in place indicated.

Beginning double shell (beg double shell): (Beg shell, ch 2, 2 dc) in place indicated.

Double shell (double shell): (Shell, ch 2, 2 dc) in place indicated.

INSTRUCTIONS

DOILY

Rnd 1: Ch 4, sl st in first ch to form a ring, **ch 3** (see Pattern Notes), 19 dc in ring, **join** (see Pattern Notes) in 3rd ch of beg ch-3. (20 dc)

Rnd 2: Ch 3, dc in same st, ch 3, sk next dc, [2 dc in next dc, ch 3, sk next dc] around, join in 3rd ch of beg ch-3. (10 ch-3 sps)

Rnd 3: Sl st in next dc and in next ch-3 sp, ch 1, (sc, **ch-3 picot**—see Special Stitches, ch 5) in same ch sp and in each ch-3 sp around, ending with sc in last ch-3 sp, ch-3 picot, join with ch 2, dc in beg sc to form last ch-5 sp. (10 ch-5 sps)

Rnd 4: Ch 1, sc in ch sp just made, [ch 7, sc in next ch-5 sp] around, ch 7, join in beg sc. (10 ch-7 sps)

Rnd 5: Ch 1, *sc in each of first 2 chs of next ch-7, 2 sc in next ch, sc in next ch, 2 sc in next ch, sc in each of next 2 chs, sl st in next sc, rep from * around, join in beg ch-1. (90 sc)

Rnd 6: Working in **back lps** (see Stitch Guide) only, sl st in each of next 4 sc, ch 5 (counts as first dc and ch-2), *(tr, ch 2) twice in next sc, (dc, ch 3) in next sc**, (dc, ch 2) in 4th sc of next 9-sc group, rep from * around, ending last rep at **, join in 3rd ch of beg ch-5.

Rnd 7: Ch 1, sc in first st, *[sc in each of next 2 chs, sc in next tr] twice, sc in each of next 2 chs, sc in next dc, sc in each of next 2 chs, **7-picot lp** (see Special Stitches), sc in next ch**, sc in next dc, rep from * around, ending last rep at **, join in beg sc.

Rnd 8: Sl st in each of next 4 sc, ch 4 (counts as first tr), tr in next sc, *ch 7, sc in 4th picot of next 7-picot lp, ch 7, sk next 5 sc**, tr in each of next 2 tr, rep from * around, ending last rep at **, join in 4th ch of beg ch-4.

Rnd 9: Ch 3, dc in same st, *ch 2, 2 dc in next tr, ch 3, sc in next ch-7 sp, ch 5, sc in next ch-7 sp, ch 3**, 2 dc in next tr, rep from * around, ending last rep at **, join in 3rd ch of beg ch-3.

Rnd 10: Sl st in next dc and in next ch-2 sp, **beg shell** (see Special Stitches) in same ch sp, *ch 3, sc in next ch-3 sp, (dc, ch 1) 5 times in next ch-5 sp, dc in same sp, sc in next ch-3 sp, ch 3**, **shell** (see Special Stitches) in next ch-2 sp, rep from * around, ending last rep at **, join in 3rd ch of beg ch-3.

Rnd 11: Sl st in next dc and in next ch-2 sp, beg shell in same ch sp, *ch 3, sk next ch-3 sp, [sc in next dc, ch 3] 6 times**, shell in ch-2 sp of next shell, rep from * around, ending last rep at **, join in 3rd ch of beg ch-3.

Rnd 12: Sl st in next dc and in next ch-2 sp, **beg double shell** (see Special Stitches) in same ch sp, *ch 3, sk next ch-3 sp, [sc in next ch-3 sp, ch 3] 5 times**, **double shell** (see Special Stitches) in ch-2 sp of next shell, rep from * around, ending last rep at **, join in 3rd ch of beg ch-3.

Rnd 13: Sl st in next dc and in next ch-2 sp, beg shell in same ch sp, ch 3, shell in next ch-2 sp, ch 3, *sk next ch-3 sp, [sc in next ch-3 sp, ch 3] 4 times**, [shell in next ch-2 sp, ch 3] twice, rep from * around, ending last rep at **, join in 3rd ch of beg ch-3.

Rnd 14: Sl st in next dc and in next ch-2 sp, beg shell in same ch sp, *ch 4, sc in next ch-3 sp, ch 4, shell in ch sp of next shell, ch 3, sk next ch-3 sp, [sc in next ch-3 sp, ch 3] 3 times**, shell in ch sp of next shell, rep from * around, ending last rep at **, join in 3rd ch of beg ch-3.

Rnd 15: Sl st in next dc and in next ch-2 sp, beg shell in same ch sp, *ch 4, sc in next ch-4 sp, ch 5, sc in next ch-4, ch 4, shell in ch sp of next shell, ch 3, sk next ch-3 sp, [sc in next ch-3 sp, ch 3] twice**, shell in ch sp of next shell, rep from * around, ending last rep at **, join in 3rd ch of beg ch-3.

Rnd 16: Sl st in next dc and in next ch-2 sp, beg shell in same ch sp, *ch 4, sc in next ch-4 sp, ch 4, sc in next ch-5 sp, 7-picot lp, ch 4, sc in next ch-4 sp, ch 4, shell in ch sp of next shell, ch 3, sk next ch-3 sp, sc in next ch-3 sp, ch 3**, shell in ch sp of next shell, rep from * around, ending last rep at **, join in 3rd ch of beg ch-3.

Rnd 17: Sl st in next dc and in next ch-2 sp, beg shell in same ch sp, *ch 5, 2 tr in next ch-4 sp, ch 7, sc in 4th picot of 7-picot lp, ch 7, sk next ch-4 sp, 2 tr in next ch-4 sp, ch 5**,

shell in ch sp of each of next 2 shells, rep from * around, ending last rep at **, shell in ch sp of next shell, join in 3rd ch of beg ch-3.

Rnd 18: Sl st in next dc and in next ch-2 sp, ch 1, sc in same ch sp, *ch 5, sc in next ch-5 sp, [ch 7, sc in next ch-7 sp] twice, ch 7, sc in next ch-5 sp, ch 5, sc in ch sp of next shell, ch 3**, sc in ch sp of next shell, rep from * around, ending last rep at **, join in beg sc.

Rnd 19: Sl st in next ch-5 sp, ch 3, 8 dc in same sp, *(sc, ch-3 picot) in next ch-7 sp, 15 dc in next ch-7 sp, (sc, ch-3 picot) in next ch-7 sp, 9 dc in next ch-5 sp, (sc, ch-3 picot) in next ch-3 sp**, 9 dc in next ch-5 sp, rep from * around, ending last rep at **, join in 3rd ch of beg ch-3. Fasten off. ❏❏

Songbird Wreath

Design by Jo Ann Maxwell

SKILL LEVEL

◖■ ■ ■ ▭

INTERMEDIATE

FINISHED SIZE
3 x 6 inches

MATERIALS
- ❑ South Maid crochet cotton size 10 (350 yds per ball): 1 ball #430 cream
- ❑ Size 5/1.90mm steel crochet hook or size needed to obtain gauge
- ❑ 1½-inch diameter plastic foam ball
- ❑ Small balloon
- ❑ ⅛-inch diameter beads or rhinestones: 2
- ❑ Small sprig gold gyposphila
- ❑ 20-inch pre-assembled floral wreath
- ❑ Fabric stiffener
- ❑ Craft glue

GAUGE
First 2 rnds of head = 1½ inches in diameter

PATTERN NOTES
Join with slip stitch as indicated unless otherwise stated.

Chain-3 at beginning of row or round counts as first double crochet unless otherwise stated.

INSTRUCTIONS

BIRD
Body
Rnd 1: Beg at top of head, ch 4, sl st in first ch to form a ring, ch 4 *(counts as first dc and ch-1)*, [dc in ring, ch 1] 11 times, **join** *(see Pattern Notes)* in 3rd ch of beg ch-4. *(12 ch-1 sps)*

Rnds 2–5: Ch 5 *(counts as first dc and ch-2)*, [dc in next dc, ch 2] around, join in 3rd ch of beg ch-5. At end of last rnd, slip plastic foam ball inside, join in 3rd ch of beg ch-5.

Rnd 6: Ch 4 *(counts as first dc and ch-1)*, [dc in next dc, ch 1] around, join in 3rd ch of beg ch-4.

Rnd 7: Ch 1, sc in first st and in each st around, join in beg sc. *(12 sc)*

Rnd 8: Ch 4 *(counts as first dc and ch-1)*, (dc, ch 1) in same st as joining, *(dc, ch 1) in next st, (dc, ch 1) twice in next st, rep from * around, ending with (dc, ch 1) in last st, join in 3rd ch of beg ch-4. *(18 ch-1 sps)*

Rnd 9: Ch 4 *(counts as first hdc and ch-2)*, [hdc in next dc, ch 2] 7 times, [dc in next dc, ch 2] 6 times, [hdc in next dc, ch 2] 4 times, join in 2nd ch of beg ch-4.

Rnds 10–15: Ch 4, [hdc in next hdc, ch 2] 7 times, [dc in next dc, ch 2] 6 times, [hdc in next hdc, ch 2] 4 times, join in 2nd ch of beg ch-4.

Rnd 16: Ch 3 *(counts as first hdc and ch-1)*, [hdc in next hdc, ch 1] 7 times, [dc in next dc, ch 1] 6 times, [hdc in next hdc, ch 1] 4 times, join in 2nd ch of beg ch-3.

Rnd 17: Ch 1, sc in each hdc and dc around, join in beg sc. *(18 sc)*

Tail
Row 18: Ch 3 *(see Pattern Notes)*, 2 dc in same st, 3 dc in each of next 3 sts, leaving rem sts unworked, turn. *(12 dc)*

Rows 19–22: Ch 4 *(counts as first dc and ch-1)*, dc in next dc, [ch 1, dc in next dc] across, turn. *(11 ch-1 sps)*

Row 23: Ch 5 *(counts as first dc and ch-2)*, dc in next dc, [ch 2, dc in next dc] across. Fasten off. *(11 ch-2 sps)*

Wing
Make 2.
Row 1: Ch 4, join to form a ring, ch 3, dc in ring, ch 1, [dc in ring, ch 1] 8 times, 2 dc in ring, turn.

Row 2: Ch 3, dc in next dc, ch 2, sc in next dc, [ch 3, sc in next dc] 7 times, ch 2, dc in each of last 2 dc, turn.

Row 3: Ch 3, dc in next dc, ch 2, sc in next ch-3 sp, [ch 3, sc in next ch-3 sp] 6 times, ch 2, dc in each of last 2 dc, turn.

Row 4: Ch 3, dc in next dc, ch 2, sc in next ch-3 sp, [ch 3, sc in next ch-3 sp] 5 times, ch 2, dc in each of last 2 dc, turn.

Row 5: Ch 3, dc in next dc, ch 2, sc in next ch-3 sp, [ch 3, sc in next ch-3 sp] 4 times, ch 2, dc in each of last 2 dc, turn.

Row 6: Ch 3, dc in next dc, ch 2, sc in next ch-3 sp, [ch 3, sc in next ch-3 sp] 3 times, ch 2, dc in each of last 2 dc, turn.

Row 7: Ch 3, dc in next dc, ch 2, sc in next ch-3 sp, [ch 3, sc in next ch-3 sp] twice, ch 2, dc in each of last 2 dc, turn.

Row 8: Ch 3, dc in next dc, ch 2, sc in next ch-3 sp, ch 3, sc in next ch-3 sp, ch 2, dc in each of last 2 dc, turn.

Row 9: Ch 3, dc in next dc, ch 2, sc in next ch-3 sp, ch 2, dc in each of last 2 dc, turn.

Row 10: Ch 3, dc in next dc, dc in each of last 2 dc, turn.

Row 11: Ch 3, sl st in last dc. Fasten off.

Beak
With 2 strands of crochet cotton held tog, ch 7. Fasten off, do not trim ends until stiffened and dried.

Finishing
Insert deflated balloon into Bird's body. Inflate balloon, dip Bird in fabric stiffener. Pin ends of Tail to cardboard covered with plastic wrap so Bird is upright. Tie piece of crochet cotton tightly around neck.

Stiffen Wings and Beak, let dry.

When Bird is dry, burst balloon and remove, crush plastic foam ball and remove.

Glue Wings on both sides of Bird as shown in photo, having pointed ends toward Tail.

Glue Beak and eyes to Bird, trimming ends of Beak.

Glue small twig from wreath in Bird's Beak.

Glue Bird to wreath as desired. ❑❑

Small Pineapple Basket

Design by Jo Ann Maxwell

FINISHED SIZE

10½ inches tall x 7½ inches wide

MATERIALS

- ❑ South Maid crochet cotton size 10 (350 yds per ball): 1 ball #42 cream
- ❑ Size 5/1.90mm steel crochet hook or size needed to obtain gauge
- ❑ 1-Inch diameter plastic foam balls: 2
- ❑ 5 yds ¼-wide green satin ribbon
- ❑ 1½-inch pink satin roses with leaves: 5
- ❑ 2 small balloons
- ❑ ⅛-inch diameter beads: 4
- ❑ 24 inches gold metallic thread
- ❑ Small amount gold gypsophila
- ❑ Vegetable can
- ❑ Mixing bowl
- ❑ Clothespin
- ❑ Fabric stiffener
- ❑ Plastic wrap
- ❑ Cardboard
- ❑ Straight pins
- ❑ Craft glue

GAUGE

First 3 rnds of basket = 3 inches in diameter

PATTERN NOTES

Join with slip stitch as indicated unless otherwise stated

Chain-3 at beginning of row or round counts as first double crochet unless otherwise stated.

JOINED SHELL STITCH PATTERN

Rnd 1: (Ch 3, dc, ch 2, dc) in indicated st, *holding back on hook last lp of each st, dc in same st as last dc, sk next 2 sts, dc in next st, yo, pull through all 3 lps on hook (joined dc completed), (dc, ch 2, dc) in same st as 2nd leg of last joined dc, rep from * around, ending with dc in same st as last dc until 2 lps on hook, insert hook in 3rd ch of beg ch-3, yo, pull through st and all lps on hook.

Rnd 2: Sl st in next dc and in ch-2 sp, ch 3, (dc, ch 2, dc) in same ch sp, *holding back on hook last lp of each st, dc in same ch sp as last dc, dc in ch sp of next shell, yo, pull through all 3 lps on hook (joined dc completed), (dc, ch 2, dc) in same ch sp as 2nd leg of last joined dc, rep from * around, ending as for rnd 1.

Rep rnd 2 for pattern.

SPECIAL STITCHES

Beginning shell (beg shell): Ch 3, (dc, ch 2, 2 dc) in indicated st or ch sp.

Shell: (2 dc, ch 2, 2 dc) in indicated st or ch sp.

Double shell: (Shell, ch 2, 2 dc) in indicated ch sp.

Picot: Ch 3, sl st in last sc.

INSTRUCTIONS

BIRD

Head
Make 2.

Rnd 1: Beg at top of head, ch 4, sl st in first ch to form ring, ch 4 (counts as first dc and ch-1), [dc in ring, ch 1] 7 times, **join** (see Pattern Notes) in 3rd ch of beg ch-4. (8 ch-1 sps)

Rnds 2 & 3: Ch 5 (counts as first dc and ch-2), [dc in next dc, ch 2] around, join in 3rd ch of beg ch-5, at end of rnd 3, slip plastic foam ball inside, join in 3rd ch of beg ch-5.

Rnd 4: Ch 4 (counts as first dc and ch-1), [dc in next dc, ch 1] around, join in 3rd ch of beg ch-4.

Rnd 5: Ch 1, dc in first st, sc in each dc around, join in beg sc. (8 sc)

Body
Make 2.

Rnd 6: Ch 5 (counts as first dc and ch-2), (dc, ch 2) in same st as joining, *(dc, ch 2) in next st, (dc, ch 2) twice in next st, rep from * around, ending with (dc, ch 2) in last st, join in 3rd ch of beg ch-5. (12 ch-2 sps)

Rnd 7: Ch 4 (counts as first hdc and ch-2), [hdc in next dc, ch 2] 4 times, [dc in next dc, ch 2] 5 times, [hdc in next dc, ch 2] twice, join in 2nd ch of beg ch-4.

Rnds 8–10: Ch 4 (counts as first hdc and ch-2), [hdc in next hdc, ch 2] 4 times, [dc in next dc, ch 2] 5 times, [hdc in next hdc, ch 2] twice, join in 2nd ch of beg ch-4.

Rnd 11: Ch 3 (counts as first hdc and ch-1), [hdc in next hdc, ch 1] 4 times, [dc in next dc, ch 1] 5 times, [hdc in next hdc, ch 1] twice, join in 2nd ch of beg ch-3.

Rnd 12: Ch 1, sc in each hdc and dc around, join in beg sc. (12 sc)

Tail
Make 2.

Row 13: Ch 3 (see Pattern Notes), 2 dc in same st, 3 dc in each of next 2 sc, leaving rem sts unworked, turn. (9 dc)

Rows 14 & 15: Ch 4 (counts as first dc and ch-1), dc in next dc, [ch 1, dc in next dc] across, turn. (8 ch-1 sps)

Row 16: Ch 5 (counts as first dc and ch-2), dc in next dc, [ch 2, dc in next dc] across. Fasten off. (8 ch-2 sps)

Wing
Make 4.

Row 1: Ch 4, dc in 4th ch from hook (first 3 chs count as first dc), ({ch 1, dc} 5 times, ch 1, 2 dc) in same ch, turn. (9 dc)

Row 2: Ch 3, dc in next dc, ch 2, sc in next dc, (ch 3, sc in next dc) 4 times, ch 2, dc in each of last 2 dc, turn.

Row 3: Ch 3, dc in next dc, ch 2, sc in next ch-3 sp, [ch 3, sc in next ch-3 sp] 3 times, ch 2, dc in each of last 2 dc, turn.

Row 4: Ch 3, dc in next dc, ch 2, sc in next ch-3 sp, [ch 3, sc in next ch-3 sp] twice, ch 2, dc in each of last 2 dc, turn.

Row 5: Ch 3, dc in next dc, ch 2, sc in next ch-3 sp, ch 3, sc in next ch-3 sp, ch 2, dc in each of last 2 dc, turn.

Row 6: Ch 3, dc in next dc, ch 2, sc in next ch-3 sp, ch 2, dc in each of last 2 dc, turn.

Row 7: Ch 3, dc in next dc, sk 2 ch-2 sps, dc in each of last 2 dc, turn.

Row 8: Ch 4, sk next 2 dc, sl st in last dc. Fasten off.

Beak
Make 2.
With 2 strands of crochet cotton held tog, ch 6. Fasten off.
Do not trim ends until stiffened and dried.

Finishing
Insert deflated balloon into Bird's body and inflate.

Dip Bird in fabric stiffener, pin ends of Tail to cardboard covered with plastic wrap so Bird is upright. Tie piece of thread tightly around neck.

Stiffen Wings and Beak, let dry.

When Bird is dry, burst balloon and remove, crush plastic foam ball and remove.

Glue Wings on both sides of Bird, having pointed ends toward Tail. Glue Beak and beads for eyes to Bird, trim ends on Beak.

Glue small sprig of gold gypsophila in Bird's Beak.

Cut 12 inch length of gold metallic thread, tie in bow around Bird's neck, trim ends.

Rep for 2nd Bird.

BASKET
Rnd 1: Ch 4, sl st in first ch to form ring, ch 3, 19 dc in ring, join in 3rd ch of beg ch-3. *(20 dc)*

Rnd 2: Ch 7 (counts as first dtr and ch-2), [dtr in next dc, ch 2] around, join in 5th ch of beg ch-7. *(20 ch-2 sps)*

Rnd 3: Ch 3, dc in each of next 2 chs, [dc in next dtr, dc in each of next 2

chs] around, join in 3rd ch of beg ch-3. *(60 dc)*

Rnd 4: Working in **back lps** (see Stitch Guide) only, beg in same st as joining, work rnd 1 of Joined Shell Stitch Pattern around. *(20 joined shells)*

Rnds 5–12: Work rnd 2 of Joined Shell Stitch Pattern.

Rnd 13: Sl st in next dc and in ch-2 sp, **beg shell** (see Special Stitches) in same ch sp, [**shell** (see Special Stitches) in ch sp of next shell] twice, *ch 1, 5 dc in ch sp of next shell, ch 1**, [shell in ch sp of next shell] 3 times, rep from * around, ending last rep at **, join in 3rd ch of beg ch-3.

Rnd 14: Sl st in next dc and in ch-2 sp, ch 1, sc in same sp, *ch 3, **double shell** (see Special Stitches) in ch sp of next shell, ch 3, sc in ch sp of next shell, dc in first dc of next 5-dc group, [ch 1, dc in next dc] 4 times, sc in ch sp of next shell, rep from * around, join in beg sc.

Rnd 15: Sl st in each of next 3 chs, next 2 dc and next ch-2 sp, beg shell in same ch sp, *ch 3, shell in next ch-2 sp, ch 3, [sc in next dc, ch 3] 5 times**, shell in next ch-2 sp, rep from * around, ending last rep at **, join in 3rd ch of beg ch-3.

Rnd 16: Sl st in next dc and in ch-2 sp, beg shell in same sp, *ch 3, sc in next ch-3 sp, ch 3, shell in ch sp of next shell, ch 3, sk next ch-3 sp, [sc in next ch-3 sp, ch 3] 4 times**, shell in ch sp of next shell, rep from * around, ending last rep at **, join in 3rd ch of beg ch-3.

Rnd 17: Sl st in next dc and in ch-2 sp, beg shell in same ch sp, *ch 3, [sc in next ch-3 sp, ch 3] twice, shell in ch sp of next shell, ch 3, sk next ch-3 sp, [sc in next ch-3 sp, ch 3] 3 times**, shell in ch sp of next shell, rep from * around, ending last rep at **, join in 3rd ch of beg ch-3.

Rnd 18: Sl st in next dc and in ch-2 sp, beg shell in same ch sp, *ch 4, [sc in next ch-3 sp, ch 4] 3 times, shell in ch sp of next shell, ch 3, sk next ch-3 sp, [sc in next ch-3 sp, ch 3] twice**, shell in ch sp of next shell, rep from * around, ending last rep at **, join in 3rd ch of beg ch-3.

Rnd 19: Sl st in next dc and in ch-2 sp, beg shell in same ch sp, *ch 4, [sc in next ch-4 sp, ch 4] 4 times, shell

in ch sp of next shell, ch 3, sk next ch-3 sp, sc in next ch-3 sp, ch 3**, shell in ch sp of next shell, rep from * around, ending last rep at **, join in 3rd ch of beg ch-3.

Rnd 20: Sl st in next dc and in ch-2 sp, beg shell in same ch sp, *ch 5, [sc in next ch-4 sp, ch 5] 5 times**, [shell in ch sp of next shell] twice, rep from * around, ending last rep at **, shell in ch sp of next shell, join in 3rd ch of beg ch-3.

Rnd 21: Sl st in next dc and in ch-2 sp, ch 1, sc in same ch sp, *[ch 5, sc in next ch-5 sp] 6 times**, [ch 5, sc in ch sp of next shell] twice, rep from * around, ending last rep at **, ch 5, sc in ch sp of next shell, ch 5, join in beg sc. *(40 ch-5 sps)*

Rnd 22: Sl st in each of next 3 chs, ch 1, [sc, picot] in same ch-5 sp, *9 dc in next ch-5 sp**, [sc, picot] in next ch-5 sp, rep from * around, ending last rep at **, join in beg sc. Fasten off.

Base
Rnd 1: Working in rem lps of rnd 3 at bottom of Basket, join with sl st in rem lp of any dc in which a rnd 4 joined shell was worked, beg shell in same sp, [sk next 2 sts, shell in next st] around, ending with sk next 2 sts, join in 3rd ch of beg ch-3.

Rnd 2: Sl st in next dc and in ch-2 sp, beg shell in same ch sp, [shell in ch sp of next shell] around, join in 3rd ch of beg ch-3.

Rnd 3: Sl st in next dc and in ch-2 sp, beg shell in same sp, ch 1, [shell in ch sp of next shell, ch 1] around, join in 3rd ch of beg ch-3.

Rnd 4: Sl st in next dc and in ch-2 sp, ch 3, 6 dc in same sp, *(sc, **picot**–see Special Stitches) in ch-1 sp, 7 dc in ch sp of next shell, rep from * around, ending with (sc, picot) in last ch-1 sp, join in 3rd ch of beg ch-3. Fasten off.

Handle
Row 1: Ch 97, hdc in 7th ch from hook, [ch 2, sk next 2 chs, hdc in next ch] across, turn.

Row 2: Ch 1, 5 sc in first ch-2 sp, [5 dc in next ch-2 sp, (sc, picot) in next ch-2 sp] across, ending with 5 dc in next-to-last ch sp, 7 sc in last ch sp, working across opposite side, 5 dc in next ch sp, [(sc, picot) in next ch sp, 5 dc in next sp] across, ending with 2 sc in same ch sp as beg 5 sc, join in beg sc. Fasten off.

Finishing

Cut 8 inch diameter circle from cardboard, cover cardboard circle and vegetable can with plastic wrap. Apply fabric stiffener to Basket, place can in Basket, place Basket on cardboard circle.

Pin Base to circle evenly around. With can still inside Basket and Base at top, place Basket over mixing bowl, shaping top of Basket evenly around bowl.

When partially dry, remove from mixing bowl, fold sides up and secure at center with clothespin, removing clothespin when sides will remain upright on their own. Finish drying.

Apply fabric stiffener to Handle, lay flat on plastic wrap, removing before it is completely dry and shaping into an arc. Finish drying.

Cut 18-inch length of ribbon, weave through sps at center of Handle. Glue ends to inside of Handle and trim.

Glue 1 inch of each end of Handle to inside of Basket.

Cut 3 pieces of ribbon each 24 inches in length. Holding all 3 lengths tog, tie into bow, glue to top of Handle

as shown in photo.

Glue 2 roses and small sprig of gold gypsophila at center of bow.

Cut 4 pieces of ribbon each 12 inches in length. Holding 2 lengths tog, tie into bow, rep.

Glue 1 bow to outside of Basket at base of Handle on each side.

Glue 1 rose and small sprig gold gypsophila at center of each bow.

Glue 1 Bird at top of Basket next to Handle, as shown in photo.

Cut 12-inch length of ribbon, wrap around bottom of Basket above Base, overlapping ends, glue ends tog.

Cut 2 pieces of ribbon each 12 inches in length. Holding both lengths tog, tie into bow, glue over ribbon at bottom of Basket at center front.

Glue 1 rose and small sprig gold gypsophila at center of bow.

Glue 2nd Bird and small sprig of gold gypsophila to base of Basket below first Bird. ❑❑

Tissue Box Cover

Design by Jo Ann Maxwell

SKILL LEVEL

■■■□

INTERMEDIATE

FINISHED SIZE

Fits boutique-style tissue box

MATERIALS

- ❑ Size 10 crochet cotton: 350 yds natural
- ❑ Size F/5/3.75mm crochet hook or size needed to obtain gauge
- ❑ ⅜-inch diameter white pearl beads: 4
- ❑ ¼-inch diameter white pearl beads: 8
- ❑ 1¼ inches wide pink satin roses with leaves: 4
- ❑ 3¾ yds ¼-wide green satin ribbon
- ❑ Craft glue
- ❑ Plastic wrap
- ❑ Spray starch

GAUGE

Rnds 1–3 = 3¼ inches in diameter

PATTERN NOTES

Join with slip stitch as indicated unless otherwise stated.

Chain-3 at beginning of row or round counts as first double crochet unless otherwise stated.

SPECIAL STITCHES

Beginning shell (beg shell): Ch 3, (dc, ch 2, 2 dc) in place indicated.

Shell: (2 dc, ch 2, 2 dc) in place indicated.

Picot: Ch 3, sl st in last sc.

Beginning double shell (beg double shell): (Beg shell, ch 2, 2 dc) in place indicated.

Double shell: (Shell, ch 2, 2 dc) in place indicated.

INSTRUCTIONS

COVER

Rnd 1: Beg at bottom, ch 4, sl st in first ch to form ring, **ch 3** *(see Pattern Notes)*, 23 dc in ring, **join** *(see Pattern Notes)* in 3rd ch of beg ch-3. *(24 dc)*

Rnd 2: Ch 7 *(counts as first dtr and ch-2)*, (dtr, ch 2) in each dc around, join in 5th ch of beg ch-7. *(24 ch-2 sps)*

Rnd 3: Ch 3, [dc in each of next 2 chs, dc in next dtr] around, ending with dc in each of last 2 chs, join in 3rd ch of beg ch-3. *(72 dc)*

Rnd 4: Ch 1, sc in first st, ch 4, [sk next dc, sc in next dc, ch 4] around, join in beg sc. *(36 ch-4 sps)*

Rnds 5–8: Sl st in each of next 2 chs, ch 1, sc in same ch sp, ch 4, [sc in next ch-4 sp, ch 4] around, join in beg sc.

Rnd 9: Sl st in next ch-4 sp, **beg double shell** *(see Special Stitches)* in same ch sp, *ch 3, sc in next ch-4 sp, [ch 4, sc in next ch-4 sp] 7 times, ch 3**, **double shell** *(see Special Stitches)* in next ch-4 sp, rep from * around, ending last rep at **, join in 3rd ch of beg ch-3.

Rnd 10: Sl st in next dc and in ch-2 sp, **beg shell** *(see Special Stitches)* in same ch sp, ch 3, **shell** *(see Special Stitches)* in next ch-2 sp, *ch 3, sk ch-3 sp, sc in next ch-4 sp, [ch 4, sc in next ch-4 sp] 6 times**, [ch 3, shell in next ch-2 sp] twice, rep from * around, ending last rep at **, ch 3, join in 3rd ch of beg ch-3.

Rnd 11: Sl st in next dc and in ch-2 sp, beg shell in same ch sp, *ch 3, 7 dc in next ch-3 sp, ch 3, shell in ch sp of next shell, ch 3, sk next ch-3 sp, sc in next ch-4 sp, [ch 4, sc in next ch-4 sp] 5 times, ch 3**, shell in ch sp of next shell, rep from * around, ending last rep at **, join in 3rd ch of beg ch-3.

Rnd 12: Sl st in next dc and in ch-2 sp, beg shell in same ch sp, *ch 3, sc in next ch-3 sp, dc in next dc, [ch 1, dc in next dc] 6 times, sc in next ch-3 sp, ch 3, shell in ch sp of next shell, ch 3, sk next ch-3 sp, sc in next ch-4 sp, [ch 4, sc in next ch-4 sp] 4 times, ch 3**, shell in ch sp of next shell, rep from * around, ending last rep at **, join in 3rd ch of beg ch-3.

Rnd 13: Sl st in next dc and in ch-2 sp, beg shell in same ch sp, *ch 3, sk next ch-3 sp, sc in next dc, ch 3] 7 times, shell in ch sp of next shell, ch 3, sk next ch-3 sp, sc in next ch-4 sp, [ch 4, sc in next ch-4 sp] 3 times, ch 3**, shell in ch sp of next shell, rep from * around, ending last rep at **, join in 3rd ch of beg ch-3.

Rnd 14: Sl st in next dc and in ch-2 sp, beg shell in same sp, *ch 3, sk next ch-3 sp, [sc in next ch-3 sp, ch 3] 6 times, shell in ch sp of next shell, ch 3, sk next ch-3 sp, sc in next ch-4 sp, [ch 4, sc in next ch-4 sp] twice, ch 3**, shell in ch sp of next shell, rep from * around, ending last rep at **, join in 3rd ch of beg ch-3.

Rnd 15: Sl st in next dc and in ch-2 sp, beg shell in same sp, *ch 3, sk next ch-3 sp, [sc in next ch-3 sp, ch 3] 5 times, shell in ch sp of next shell, ch 4, sc in next ch-3 sp, [ch 4, sc in next ch-4 sp] twice, ch 4, sc in next ch-3 sp, ch 4**, shell in ch sp of next shell, rep from * around, ending last rep at **, join in 3rd ch of beg ch-3.

Rnd 16: Sl st in next dc and in ch-2 sp, beg shell in same ch sp, *ch 3, sk next ch-3 sp, [sc in next ch-3 sp, ch 3] 4 times, shell in ch sp of next shell, ch 4, [sc in next ch-4 sp, ch 4] 5 times**, shell in ch sp of next shell, rep from * around, ending last rep at **, join in 3rd ch of beg ch-3.

Rnd 17: Sl st in next dc and in ch-2 sp, beg shell in same ch sp, *ch 3, sk next ch-3 sp, [sc in next ch-3 sp, ch 3] 3 times, shell in ch sp of next shell, ch 4, [sc in next ch-4 sp, ch 4] 6 times**, shell in ch sp of next shell, rep from * around, ending last rep at **, join in 3rd ch of beg ch-3.

Rnd 18: Sl st in next dc and in ch-2 sp, beg shell in same ch sp, *ch 3, sk next ch-3 sp, [sc in next ch-3 sp, ch 3] twice, shell in ch sp of next shell, ch 4, [sc in next ch-4 sp, ch 4] 7 times**, shell in ch sp of next shell, rep from * around, ending last rep at **, join in 3rd ch of beg ch-3.

Rnd 19: Sl st in next dc and in ch-2 sp, beg shell in same ch sp, *ch 3, sk next ch-3 sp, sc in next ch-3 sp, ch

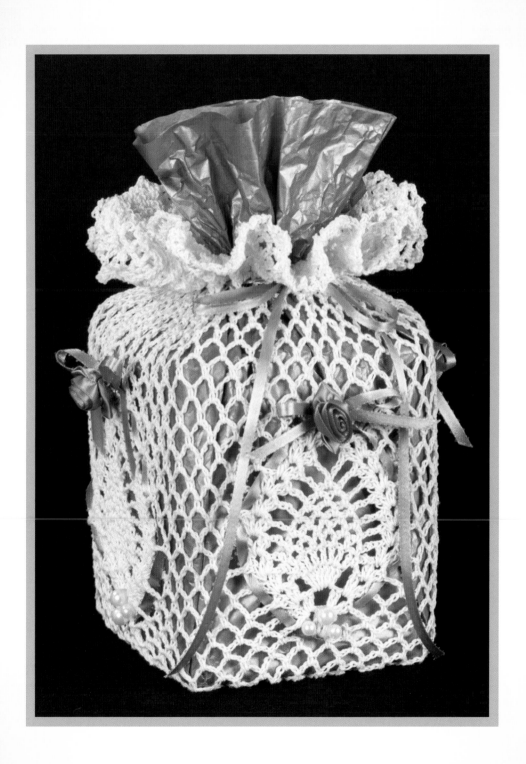

3, shell in ch sp of next shell, ch 4, [sc in next ch-4 sp, ch 4] 8 times**, shell in ch sp of next shell, rep from * around, ending last rep at **, join in 3rd ch of beg ch-3.

Rnd 20: Sl st in next dc and in ch-2 sp, beg shell in same sp, shell in ch sp of next shell, *ch 4, [sc in next ch-4 sp, ch 4] 9 times**, shell in ch sp of each of next 2 shells, rep from * around, ending last rep at **, join in 3rd ch of beg ch-3.

Rnd 21: Sl st in next dc and in ch-2 sp, ch 1, sc in same ch sp, sc in ch sp of next shell, *ch 4, [sc in next ch-4 sp, ch 4] 10 times**, sc in ch sp of each of next 2 shells, rep from * around, ending last rep at **, join in beg sc.

Rnd 22: Sl st in next sc and in each of next 2 chs, ch 1, sc in same sp, ch 4, [sc in next ch-4 sp, ch 4] around, join in beg sc. *(44 ch-4 sps)*

Rnds 23–27: Sl st in each of next 2 chs, ch 1, sc in same ch sp, ch 4, [sc in next ch-4 sp, ch 4] around, join in beg sc.

Rnd 28: Sl st in each of next 2 chs, ch 6 *(counts as first dc and ch-3)*, [dc in next ch-4 sp, ch 3] around, join in 3rd ch of beg ch-6.

Rnd 29: Ch 1, sc in first st, ch 4, [sc in next ch-3 sp, ch 4, sc in next dc, ch 4] around, ending with sc in last ch-3 sp, ch 4, join in beg sc. *(88 ch-4 sps)*

Rnds 30–35: Sl st in each of next 2 chs, ch 1, sc in same sp, ch 4, [sc in next ch-4 sp, ch 4] around, join in beg sc.

Rnd 36: Sl st in next ch, ch 5 *(counts as first dc and ch-2)*, *[dc in next ch, ch 2] 3 times, sc in next ch-4 sp, ch 2**, dc in first ch of next ch-4, ch 2, rep from * around, ending last rep at **, join in 3rd ch of beg ch-5. Fasten off.

Finishing

Cover tissue box with plastic wrap, place crocheted Cover over box, centering Pineapples over 4 sides. Gather top with string woven through sps of rnd 28. Pull string tightly, leaving sp for tissue to come out. Shape ruffle, spray with starch. Let dry.

Remove crocheted Cover. Cut 4 pieces of ribbon each 24 inches long. Beg at top of each Pineapple, weave ribbon through sps at outer edge of shells around each of 4 Pineapples, tie in bow at top and trim ends.

Glue satin rose to center of each bow. Glue 2 small pearl beads and 1 large pearl bead at base of each Pineapple over double shell.

Place Cover on box, centering pineapples over 4 sides. Weave rem piece of ribbon through sps of rnd 28, gather and tie in bow. Trim ends to desired length. ❏❏

Mirror Image Doily

Design by Diane Poellot

SKILL LEVEL

INTERMEDIATE

FINISHED SIZE
7 x 18 inches

MATERIALS
- ❑ Size 20 crochet cotton:
  150 yds crystal blue
- ❑ Size 8/1.50mm steel crochet
  hook or size needed to
  obtain gauge
- ❑ Starch

GAUGE
3 shell rnds = 1 inch

PATTERN NOTES

Join with slip stitch as indicated unless otherwise stated.

When a round begins with a shell, slip stitch in chain space and work a beginning shell as stated in Special Stitches.

Chain-3 at beginning of row or round counts as first double crochet unless otherwise stated.

SPECIAL STITCHES

Beginning shell (beg shell): Ch 3, (dc, ch 2, 2 dc) in place indicated.

Shell: (2 dc, ch 2, 2 dc) in place indicated.

Picot: Ch 3, sl st in first ch of ch-3.

Double crochet picot shell (dc picot shell): ({2 dc, picot} 3 times, 2 dc) in place indicated.

INSTRUCTIONS
DOILY

Rnd 1: Ch 10, sl st in first ch to form ring, **ch 3** (see Pattern Notes), dc in ring, [ch 2, (2 dc, ch 1, 2 dc) in ring] 3 times, ch 2, 2 dc in ring, ch 1, **join** (see Pattern Notes) in 3rd ch of beg ch-3. (16 dc, 8 ch sps)

Rnd 2: Beg shell (see Pattern Note) in ch-2 sp, *ch 3, dc in ch-1 sp, ch 3**, **shell** (see Special Stitches) in next ch-2 sp, rep from * around, ending last rep at **, join.

Rnd 3: [Shell in ch-2 sp of next shell, ch 3, (dc, ch 5, dc) in next single dc between shells, ch 3] around, join.

Rnd 4: [Shell in ch-2 sp of next shell, ch 3, 9 tr in next ch-5 sp, ch 3] around, join in 3rd ch of beg ch-3. *(4 pineapple bases, 4 shells)*

Rnd 5: *Shell in ch-2 sp of next shell, ch 3, tr in first tr of 9-tr group, [ch 1, tr in next tr] 8 times, ch 3, rep from * around, join in 3rd ch of beg ch-3.

Rnd 6: *Shell in ch-2 sp of next shell, ch 4, sc in next ch-1 sp, [ch 3, sc in next ch-1 sp] 7 times, ch 4, rep from * around, join in 3rd ch of beg ch-3.

First Half

Row 7: Beg shell in ch-2 sp of next shell, *ch 4, sc in next ch-3 sp, [ch 3, sc in next ch-3 sp] 6 times, ch 4*, (2 dc, ch 4, 2 dc) in next ch-2 sp of next shell, rep between * once, shell

in ch-2 sp of next shell, leaving rem stitches unworked, turn.

Row 8: Beg shell in ch-2 sp of next shell, *ch 4, sc in next ch-3 sp, [ch 3, sc in next ch-3 sp] 5 times, ch 4*, (shell, ch 2, shell) in next ch-4 sp, rep between * once, shell in ch-2 sp of next shell, turn.

Row 9: Beg shell in ch-2 sp of next shell, *ch 4, sc in next ch-3 sp, [ch 3, sc in next ch-3 sp] 4 times, ch 4*, [shell in ch-2 sp of next shell, ch 1] twice, shell in ch-2 sp of next shell, rep between * once, shell in ch-2 sp of next shell, turn.

Row 10: Beg shell in ch-2 sp of next shell, *ch 4, sc in next ch-3 sp, [ch 3, sc in next ch-3 sp] 3 times, ch 4 *, [shell in ch-2 sp of next shell, ch 3, dc in next ch-1 sp, ch 3] twice, shell in ch-2 sp of next shell, rep between * once, shell in ch-2 sp of next shell, turn.

Row 11: Beg shell in ch-2 sp of next

shell, *ch 4, sc in next ch-3 sp, [ch 3, sc in next ch-3 sp] twice, ch 4*, [shell in next ch-2 sp of next shell, ch 3, (dc, ch 5, dc) in single dc between shells, ch 3] twice, shell in ch-2 sp of next shell, rep between * once, shell in ch-2 sp of next shell, turn.

Row 12: Beg shell in ch-2 sp of next shell, *ch 4, sc in next ch-3 sp, ch 3, sc in next ch-3 sp, ch 4, shell in ch-2 sp of next shell*, ch 3, 9 tr in next ch-5 sp, ch 3, shell in ch-2 sp of next shell, ch 3, 9 tr in next ch-5 sp, ch 3, shell in next ch-2 sp of next shell, rep between * once, turn.

Row 13: Beg shell in ch-2 sp of next shell, *ch 4, sc in next ch-3 sp, ch 4, shell in next ch-2 sp of next shell*, **ch 3, tr in first tr of next 9-tr group, [ch 1, tr in next tr] 8 times, ch 3, shell in ch-2 sp of next shell, rep from ** once, rep between * once, turn.

Row 14: Beg shell in ch-2 sp of next shell, shell in ch-2 sp of next shell, *ch 4, sc in next ch-1 sp, [ch 3, sc in next ch-1 sp] 7 times, ch 4*, (2 dc, ch 4, 2 dc) in ch-2 sp of next shell, rep between * once, shell in ch-2 sp of each of next 2 shells, turn.

Row 15: Sl st in ch-2 sp of next shell, ch 2, shell in next ch-2 sp of next shell, *ch 4, sc in next ch-3 sp, [ch 3, sc in next ch-3 sp] 6 times, ch 4*, (shell, ch 2, shell) in ch-2 sp of next shell, rep between * once, shell in ch-2 sp of next shell, hdc in ch-2 sp of next shell, turn.

Row 16: Beg shell in ch-2 sp of next shell, *ch 4, sc in next ch-3 sp, [ch 3, sc in next ch-3 sp] 5 times, ch 4*, shell in ch-2 sp next of shell, [ch 1, shell in ch-2 sp of next shell] twice, rep between * once, shell in ch-2 sp of next shell, turn.

Row 17: Beg shell in ch-2 sp of next shell, *ch 4, sc in next ch-3 sp, [ch 3, sc in next ch-3 sp] 4 times, ch 4*, shell in ch-2 sp of next shell, [ch 2, shell in ch-2 sp of next shell] twice, rep between * once, shell in ch-2 sp of next shell, turn.

Row 18: Beg shell in ch-2 sp of next shell, *ch 4, sc in next ch-3 sp, [ch 3, sc in next ch-3 sp] 3 times, ch 4, shell in ch-2 sp of next shell*, ch 3, (shell, ch 2, 2 dc) in ch-2 sp of next shell, ch 3, shell in ch-2 sp of next shell, rep between * once, turn.

Row 19: Beg shell in ch-2 sp of next shell, *ch 4, sc in next ch-3 sp, [ch 3, sc in next ch-3 sp] twice*, [ch 4, shell in next ch-2 sp of next shell] twice, ch 1, [shell in ch-2 sp of next shell, ch 4] twice, rep between * once, ch 4, shell in ch-2 sp of next shell, turn.

Row 20: Beg shell in ch-2 sp of next shell, *ch 4, sc in next ch-3 sp, ch 3, sc in next ch-3 sp*, [ch 4, shell in ch-2 sp of next shell] 4 times, rep between * once, ch 4, shell in ch-2 sp of next shell, turn.

Row 21: Beg shell in ch-2 sp of next shell, ch 4, sc in next ch-3 sp, [ch 4, shell in ch-2 sp of next shell] 4 times, ch 4, sc in next ch-3 sp, ch 4, shell in ch-2 sp of next shell, turn. *(6 shells)*

Row 22: Beg shell in ch-2 sp of next shell, [shell in ch-2 sp of next shell, shell in next ch-4 sp] 3 times, [shell in ch-2 sp of next shell] twice, turn. *(9 shells)*

Row 23 (RS): Sl st in ch-2 sp of next shell, [ch 2, shell in ch-2 sp of next shell, ch 1] 6 times, hdc in ch-2 sp of last shell. Fasten off. *(7 shells)*

2nd Half
Row 7 (RS): Join crystal blue in same ch-2 sp of shell at edge of rnd 6, beg shell in same ch-2 sp, *ch 4, sc in next ch-3 sp, [ch 3, sc in next ch-3 sp] 6 times, ch 4*, (2 dc, ch 4, 2 dc) in ch-2 sp of next shell, rep between *, shell in ch-2 sp of next shell of rnd 6, turn.

Rows 8–23: Rep rows 8–23 of First Half.

Trim
Rnd 1 (RS): Join crystal blue in same ch-2 sp of shell at side edge in rnd 6, ch 7 *(counts as first dc and ch-4)*, dc in same ch-2 sp, *working in end of rows, ch 4, sk row 7, sc in end of next row, [ch 4, sc in end of next row] 14 times, ch 4, shell in ch-2 sp of next shell, [ch 2, shell in ch-2 sp of next shell] 6 times, [ch 4, sc in end of next row] 15 times, ch 4*, (dc, ch 4, dc) in ch-2 sp of next shell of rnd 6, rep between * once, join in 3rd ch of beg ch-7.

Rnd 2 (RS): Sl st into ch-4 sp, (ch 3, dc, **picot**—see Special Stitches, {2 dc, picot} twice, 2 dc) in same ch-4 sp, ch 2, *sk next ch-4 sp, (sc, picot, sc) in next sc, ch 2, sk next ch-4 sp, **dc picot shell** *(see Special Stitches)* in next ch-4 sp, ch 2*, rep between * 4 times, (sc, picot, sc) in next ch-4 sp, ch 2, **dc picot shell in next ch-2 sp of shell, ch 2, (sc, picot, sc) in next ch sp between shells, ch 2**, rep between ** 6 times, dc picot shell in next ch-4 sp, ch 2, rep between * 10 times, (sc, picot, sc) in next ch-4 sp, ch 2, rep between ** 7 times, dc picot shell in next ch-4 sp, ch 2, rep between * 4 times, sk next ch-4 sp, (sc, picot, sc) in next sc, ch 2, join in 3rd ch of beg ch-7. Fasten off. *(36 dc picot shells)*

Starch lightly and press. ❑❑

Square Pineapple Doily

Design by Jo Ann Maxwell

SKILL LEVEL

■■■□

INTERMEDIATE

FINISHED SIZE

20 inches square

MATERIALS

❑ South Maid crochet cotton size 10 (350 yds per ball): 2 balls #430 cream
❑ Size 5/1.90mm steel crochet hook or size needed to obtain gauge

GAUGE

Rnds 1–10 = 3¾ inches in diameter

PATTERN NOTES

Join with slip stitch as indicated unless otherwise stated.

Chain-3 at beginning of row or round counts as first double crochet unless otherwise stated.

SPECIAL STITCHES

Chain-3 picot (ch-3 picot): Ch 3, sl st in last sc.

Beginning shell (beg shell): Ch 3 (see Pattern Notes), (dc, ch 2, 2 dc) in place indicated.

Shell: (2 dc, ch 2, 2 dc) in place indicated.

Beginning double shell (beg double shell): (Beg shell, ch 2, 2 dc) in place indicated.

Double shell (double shell): (Shell, ch 2, 2 dc) in place indicated.

INSTRUCTIONS
DOILY

Rnd 1: Ch 4, sl st in first ch to form ring, ch 1, 8 sc in ring, **join** (see Pattern Notes) in beg sc. (8 sc)

Rnd 2: Ch 1, sc in same st, ch 2, [sc in next sc, ch 2] around, join in beg sc. (8 ch-2 sps)

Rnd 3: Sl st in first ch-2 sp, ch 1, (sc, 4 dc, sc) in same ch sp and in each ch-2 sp around, join from behind in beg sc of rnd 2. (8 petals)

Rnd 4: Ch 1, sc in first st, ch 3, [working behind petals of rnd 3, sc in next sc of rnd 2, ch 3] around, join in beg sc. (8 ch-3 sps)

Rnd 5: Sl st in first ch-3 sp, ch 1, (sc, 6 dc, sc) in same ch sp and in each ch-3 sp around, join from behind in beg sc of rnd 4. (8 petals)

Rnd 6: Ch 1, sc in first st, ch 4, [working behind petals of rnd 5, sc in next sc of rnd 4, ch 4] around, join in beg sc. (8 ch-4 sps)

Rnd 7: Sl st in first ch-4 sp, ch 1, (sc, 9 dc, sc) in same ch sp and in each ch-4 sp around, join from behind in beg sc of rnd 6.

Rnd 8: Ch 1, sc in first, ch 6, [working behind petals of rnd 7, sc in next sc of rnd 6, ch 5] around, join in beg sc. (8 ch-5 sps)

Rnd 9: Sl st in 3rd ch of first ch-5 sp, **beg shell** (see Special Stitches) in same ch, ch 5, [**shell** (see Special Stitches) in 3rd ch of next ch-5 sp, ch 5] around, join in 3rd ch of beg ch-3. (8 shells)

Rnd 10: Sl st in next dc and in ch-2 sp, beg shell in same ch sp, *ch 3, sc in next ch-5 sp, **ch-3 picot** (see Special Stitches), ch 3**, shell in ch sp of next shell, rep from * around, ending last rep at **, join in 3rd ch of beg ch-3.

Rnd 11: Sl st in next dc and in ch-2 sp, beg shell in same ch sp, ch 9, [shell in ch sp of next shell, ch 9] around, join in 3rd ch of beg ch-3.

Rnd 12: Sl st in next dc and in ch-2 sp, ch 1, sc in same ch sp, ch-3 picot, *ch 2, sk first ch of next ch-9 sp, [dc in next ch, ch 2] 6 times, dc in next ch, ch 2**, sc in ch sp of next shell, ch-3 picot, rep from * around, ending last rep at **, join in beg sc.

Rnd 13: Sl st in each of next 2 chs and in next dc, ch 3, *[dc in each of next 2 chs, dc in next dc] 6 times, sk next ch-3 picot**, dc in next dc, rep from * around, ending last rep at **, join in 3rd ch of beg ch-3.

Rnd 14: Sl st in each of next 3 dc, beg shell in same dc, *[ch 4, sk next 5 dc, shell in next dc] twice, ch 2, sk next 6 dc**, shell in next dc, rep from * around, ending last rep at **, join in 3rd ch of beg ch-3.

Rnd 15: Sl st in next dc and in ch-2 sp, beg shell in same ch sp, *ch 3, sc in next ch-4 sp, 10 dc in ch sp of next shell, sc in next ch-4 sp, ch 3, shell in next shell, ch 2**, shell in ch sp of next shell, rep from * around, ending last rep at **, join in 3rd ch of beg ch-3.

Rnd 16: Sl st in next dc and in ch-2 sp, beg shell in same ch sp, *ch 3, sc in next ch-3 sp, [dc in next dc, ch 1] 9 times, dc in next dc, sc in next ch-3 sp, ch 3, shell in ch sp of next shell, ch 2**, shell in ch sp of next shell, rep from * around, ending last rep at **, join in 3rd ch of beg ch-3.

Rnd 17: Sl st in next dc and in ch-2 sp, beg shell in same ch sp, *ch 3, sk next ch-3 sp, sc in next dc, [ch 3, sc in next dc] 9 times, ch 3, shell in ch sp of next shell, ch 2**, shell in ch sp of next shell, rep from * around, ending last rep at **, join in 3rd ch of beg ch-3.

Rnd 18: Sl st in next dc and in ch-2 sp, beg shell in same sp, *ch 3, sk next ch-3 sp, [sc in next ch-3 sp, ch 3] 9 times, shell in ch sp of next shell, ch 2**, shell in ch sp of next shell, rep from * around, ending last rep at **, join in 3rd ch of beg ch-3.

Rnd 19: Sl st in next dc and in ch-2 sp, beg shell in same ch sp, *ch 3, sk next ch-3 sp, [sc in next ch-3 sp, ch 3] 8 times, shell in ch sp of next shell, ch 3, sc in next ch-2 sp, ch 3**, shell in ch sp of next shell, rep from * around, ending last rep at **, join in 3rd ch of beg ch-3.

Rnd 20: Sl st in next dc and in ch-2 sp, beg shell in same ch sp, *ch 3, sk next ch-3 sp, [sc in next ch-3 sp, ch 3] 7 times, shell in ch sp of next shell, [ch 3, sc in next ch-3 sp] twice, ch 3**, shell in ch sp of next shell, rep from * around, ending last rep at **, join in 3rd ch of beg ch-3.

Rnd 21: Sl st in next dc and in ch-2 sp, beg shell in same ch sp, *ch 3, sk next ch-3 sp, [sc in next ch-3 sp, ch 3] 6 times, shell in ch sp of next shell, ch 4, [sc in next ch-3 sp, ch 4] 3 times**, shell in ch sp of next shell,

rep from * around, ending last rep at **, join in 3rd ch of beg ch-3.

Rnd 22: Sl st in next dc and in ch-2 sp, beg shell in same ch sp, *ch 3, sk next ch-3 sp, [sc in next ch-3 sp, ch 3] 5 times, shell in ch sp of next shell, ch 5, [sc in next ch-4 sp, ch 5] 4 times**, shell in ch sp of next shell, rep from * around, ending last rep at **, join in 3rd ch of beg ch-3.

Rnd 23: Sl st in next dc and in ch-2 sp, beg shell in same ch sp, *ch 3, sk next ch-3 sp, [sc in next ch-3 sp, ch 3] 4 times, shell in ch sp of next shell, ch 5, [sc in next ch-5 sp, ch 5] 5 times**, shell in ch sp of next shell, rep from * around, ending last rep at **, join in 3rd ch of beg ch-3.

Rnd 24: Sl st in next dc and in ch-2 sp, beg shell in same sp, *ch 3, sk next ch-3 sp, [sc in next ch-3 sp, ch 3] 3 times, shell in ch sp of next shell, ch 5, [sc in next ch-5 sp, ch 5] 6 times**, shell in ch sp of next shell, rep from * around, ending last rep at **, join in 3rd ch of beg ch-3.

Rnd 25: Sl st in next dc and in ch-2 sp, beg shell in same ch sp, *ch 3, sk next ch-3 sp, [sc in next ch-3 sp, ch 3] twice, shell in ch sp of next shell, ch 5, [sc in next ch-5 sp, ch 5] 7 times**, shell in ch sp of next shell, rep from * around, ending last rep at **, join in 3rd ch of beg ch-3.

Rnd 26: Sl st in next dc and in ch-2 sp, beg shell in same ch sp, *ch 3, sk next ch-3 sp, sc in next ch-3 sp, ch 3, shell in ch sp of next shell, ch 5, [sc in next ch-5 sp, ch 5] 8 times**, shell in ch sp of next shell, rep from * around, ending last rep at **, join in 3rd ch of beg ch-3.

Rnd 27: Sl st in next dc and in ch-2 sp, beg shell in same ch sp, shell in ch sp of next shell, *ch 5, sc in next ch-5 sp, ch 3, **double shell** (see Special Stitches) in next ch-5 sp, ch 3, sc in next ch-5 sp, [ch 5, sc in next ch-5 sp] 4 times, ch 3, double shell in next ch-5 sp, ch 3, sc in next ch-5 sp, ch 5, shell in ch sp of each of next 2 shells, ch 5, [sc in next ch-5 sp, ch 5] 9 times**, shell in ch sp of each of next 2 shells, rep from * around, ending last rep at **, join in 3rd ch of beg ch-3.

Rnd 28: Sl st in next dc and in ch-2 sp, ch 1, sc in same ch sp, sc in ch

sp of next shell, *ch 5, sc in next ch-5 sp, ch 3, [shell in next ch-2 sp, ch 3] twice, sc in next ch-5 sp, [ch 5, sc in next ch-5 sp] 3 times, ch 3, [shell in next ch-2 sp, ch 3] twice, sc in next ch-5 sp, ch 5, sc in ch sp of each of next 2 shells, [ch 5, sc in next ch-5 sp] 10 times, ch 5**, sc in ch sp of each of next 2 shells, rep from * around, ending last rep at **, join in beg sc.

Rnd 29: Sl st in next sc and in each of next 3 chs, ch 1, sc in same ch, ◊*ch 3, shell in ch sp of next shell, ch 3, sc in next ch-3 sp, ch-3 picot, ch 3, shell in ch sp of next shell, ch 3, sc in next ch-5 sp*, [ch 5, sc in next ch-5 sp] twice, rep between * once, [ch 5, sc in next ch-5 sp] 12 times, rep from ◊ around, join in beg sc.

Rnd 30: Sl st in each of next 3 chs, next 2 dc and next ch-2 sp, beg shell in same ch sp, ◊*ch 3, sc in next ch-3 sp, ch 5, sc in next ch-3 sp, ch 3, shell in ch sp of next shell, ch 3, sc in next ch-5 sp*, ch 5, sc in next ch-5 sp, ch 3, shell in ch sp of next shell, rep between * once, [ch 5, sc in next ch-5 sp] 11 times, ch 3◊◊, shell in ch sp of next shell, rep from ◊ around, ending last rep at ◊◊, join in 3rd ch of beg ch-3.

Rnd 31: Sl st in next dc and in ch-2 sp, beg shell in same ch sp, ◊*ch 3, sc in next ch-3 sp, 8 dc in next ch-5 sp, sc in next ch-3 sp, ch 3, shell in ch sp of next shell*, ch 5, sc in next ch-5 sp, ch 5, shell in ch sp of next shell, rep between * once, ch 3, sc in next ch-5 sp, [ch 5, sc in next ch-5 sp] 10 times, ch 3◊◊, shell in ch sp of next shell, rep from ◊ around, ending last rep at ◊◊, join in 3rd ch of beg ch-3.

Rnd 32: Sl st in next dc and in ch-2 sp, beg shell in same ch sp, ◊*ch 3, sc in next ch-3 sp, (dc, ch 1) in each of next 7 dc, dc in next dc, sc in next ch-3 sp, ch 3, shell in ch sp of next shell, ch 3, sc in next ch-5 sp*, ch 5, sc in next ch-5 sp, ch 3, shell in ch sp of next shell, rep between * once, [ch 5, sc in next ch-5 sp] 9 times, ch 3◊◊, shell in ch sp of next shell, rep from ◊ around, ending last rep at ◊◊, join in 3rd ch of beg ch-3.

Rnd 33: Sl st in next dc and in ch-2 sp, beg shell in same ch sp, ◊*ch 3, sk

next ch-3 sp, [sc in next dc, ch 3] 8 times, shell in ch sp of next shell, ch 5*, shell in next ch-5 sp, ch 5, shell in ch sp of next shell, rep between * once, sk next ch-3 sp, sc in next ch-5 sp, [ch 5, sc in next ch-5 sp] 8 times, ch 5◊◊, shell in ch sp of next shell, rep from ◊ around, ending last rep at ◊◊, join in 3rd ch of beg ch-3.

Rnd 34: Sl st in next dc and in ch-2 sp, beg shell in same ch sp, ◊*ch 3, sk next ch-3 sp, [sc in next ch-3 sp, ch 3] 7 times, shell in ch sp of next shell, ch 5, sc in next ch-5 sp*, 10 dc in ch sp of next shell, sc in next ch-5 sp, ch 5, shell in ch sp of next shell, rep between * once, [ch 5, sc in next ch-5 sp] 9 times, ch 5◊◊, shell in ch sp of next shell, rep from ◊ around, ending last rep at ◊◊, join in 3rd ch of beg ch-3.

Rnd 35: Sl st in next dc and in ch-2 sp, beg shell in same ch sp, ◊*ch 3, sk next ch-3 sp, [sc in next ch-3 sp, ch 3] 6 times*, double shell in ch sp of next shell, ch 3, sc in next ch-5 sp, [dc, ch 1] in each of next 9 dc, dc in next dc, sc in next ch-5 sp, ch 3, double shell in ch sp of next shell, rep between * once, shell in ch sp of next shell, ch 5, [sc in next ch-5 sp, ch 5] 11 times◊◊, shell in ch sp of next shell, rep from ◊ around, ending last rep at ◊◊, join in 3rd ch of beg ch-3.

Rnd 36: Sl st in next dc and in ch-2 sp, beg shell in same ch sp, ◊*ch 3, sk next ch-3 sp, [sc in next ch-3 sp, ch 3] 5 times*, [shell in next ch-2 sp] twice, ch 3, sk next ch-3 sp, [sc in next dc, ch 3] 10 times, [shell in next ch-2 sp] twice, rep between * once, shell in ch sp of next shell, ch 5, [sc in next ch-5 sp, ch 5] 12 times◊◊, shell in ch sp of next shell, rep from ◊ around, ending last rep at ◊◊, join in 3rd ch of beg ch-3.

Rnd 37: Sl st in next dc and in ch-2 sp, beg shell in same sp, ch 3, ◊*sk next ch-3 sp, [sc in next ch-3 sp, ch 3] 4 times*, [shell in ch sp of next shell, ch 3] twice, sk next ch-3 sp, [sc in next ch-3 sp, ch 3] 9 times, [shell in ch sp of next shell, ch 3] twice, rep between * once, shell in ch sp of next shell, ch 3, sc in next ch-5 sp, ch-3 picot, [(dc, ch 1) 6 times in next ch-5 sp, dc in same ch sp, sc in next ch sp, ch-3 picot] 6 times, ch 3◊◊, shell in ch sp of next shell, ch 3, rep from ◊ around, ending last rep at ◊◊, join in 3rd ch of beg ch-3.

First Corner/First Pineapple
Row 38: Now working in rows, sl st in next dc and in ch-2 sp, beg shell in same ch sp, ch 3, sk next ch-3 sp, [sc in next ch-3 sp, ch 3] 3 times, shell in ch sp of next shell, leaving rem sts unworked, turn.

Row 39: Ch 3, shell in ch sp of first shell, ch 3, sk next ch-3 sp, [sc in next ch-3 sp, ch 3] twice, shell in ch sp of next shell, turn.

Row 40: Ch 3, shell in ch sp of first shell, ch 3, sk next ch-3 sp, sc in next ch-3 sp, ch 3, shell in ch sp of next shell, turn.

Row 41: Ch 3, shell in ch sp of first shell, shell in ch sp of next shell. Fasten off.

Center Pineapple
Row 38: With RS facing, join in ch sp of next unworked shell on rnd 37, beg shell in same ch sp, ch 3, sk next ch-3 sp, [sc in next ch-3 sp, ch 3] 8 times, shell in ch sp of next shell, leaving rem sts unworked, turn.

Row 39: Ch 3, shell in ch sp of first shell, ch 3, sk next ch-3 sp, [sc in next ch-3 sp, ch 3] 7 times, shell in ch sp of next shell, turn.

Row 40: Ch 3, shell in ch sp of first shell, ch 3, sk next ch-3 sp, [sc in next ch-3 sp, ch 3] 6 times, shell in ch sp of next shell, turn.

Row 41: Ch 3, shell in ch sp of first shell, ch 3, sk next ch-3 sp, [sc in next ch-3 sp, ch 3] 5 times, shell in ch sp of next shell, turn.

Row 42: Ch 3, shell in ch sp of first shell, ch 3, sk next ch-3 sp, [sc in next ch-3 sp, ch 3] 4 times, shell in ch sp of next shell, turn.

Row 43: Ch 3, shell in ch sp of first shell, ch 3, sk next ch-3 sp, [sc in next ch-3 sp, ch 3] 3 times, shell in ch sp of next shell, turn.

Rows 44–46: Rep rows 39–41 of First Corner/First Pineapple. Fasten off.

3rd Pineapple
Row 38: With RS facing, join in ch sp of next unworked shell on rnd 37, beg shell in same ch sp, ch 3, sk next ch-3 sp, [sc in next ch-3 sp, ch 3] 3 times, shell in ch sp of next shell, turn.

Rows 39–41: Rep rows 39–41 of First Corner/First Pineapple.

Rem Corners
With RS facing, join in ch sp of next unworked shell of rnd 37, rep rows 38–41 of First Corner/First Pineapple, Center Pineapple and 3rd Pineapple for each corner. ❑❑

Pineapple Runner

Design by Jo Ann Maxwell

INTERMEDIATE

FINISHED SIZE
17 inches wide x 34 inches long

MATERIALS
- ❑ South Maid crochet cotton size 10 (350 yds per ball):
  2 balls #430 cream
- ❑ Size 5/1.90mm steel crochet hook or size needed to obtain gauge

GAUGE
Rnds 1 & 2 = 2½ inches in diameter

PATTERN NOTES
Join with slip stitch as indicated unless otherwise stated.

Chain-3 at beginning of row or round counts as first double crochet unless otherwise stated.

SPECIAL STITCHES
Picot: Ch 3, sl st in last sc.

Beginning shell (beg shell): Ch 3 (see Pattern Notes), (dc, ch 2, 2 dc) in place indicated.

Shell: (2 dc, ch 2, 2 dc) in place indicated.

INSTRUCTIONS
RUNNER
Inner Section
Rnd 1: Ch 12, sl st in first ch to form ring, ch 4 (counts as first tr), tr in same st as joining, ch 3, [2 tr in next ch, ch 3] around, **join** (see Pattern Notes) in 4th ch of beg ch-4. (24 tr)

Rnd 2: Sl st in next tr and in next ch-3 sp, **beg shell** (see Special Stitches) in same ch sp, *ch 3, sc in next ch sp, ch 5, sc in next ch sp, ch 3**, **shell** (see Special Stitches) in next ch sp, rep from * around, ending last rep at **, join in 3rd ch of beg ch-3.

Rnd 3: Sl st in next dc and in ch-2 sp, beg shell in same ch sp, *ch 3, sc in next ch-3 sp, 12 dc in next ch-5 sp, sc in next ch-3 sp, ch 3, shell in ch sp of next shell, ch 7, sc in next ch-5 sp, ch 7**, shell in ch sp of next shell, rep from * around, ending last rep at **, join in 3rd ch of beg ch-3.

Complete First Inner Pineapple
Row 4 (RS): Now working in rows, sl st in next dc and in ch-2 sp, beg shell in same ch sp, ch 3, sk next ch-3 sp, tr in next dc, [ch 1, tr in next dc] 11 times, ch 3, shell in ch sp of next shell, leaving rem sts unworked, turn.

Row 5: Ch 3, shell in ch sp of first shell, ch 3, sc in next tr, [ch 4, sc in next tr] 11 times, ch 3, shell in ch sp of next shell, turn.

Row 6: Ch 3, shell in ch sp of first shell, ch 3, sk next ch-3 sp, sc in next ch-4 sp, [ch 4, sc in next ch-4 sp] 10 times, ch 3, shell in ch sp of next shell, turn.

Row 7: Ch 3, shell in ch sp of first shell, ch 3, sk next ch-3 sp, sc in next ch-4 sp, [ch 4, sc in next ch-4 sp] 9 times, ch 3, shell in ch sp of next shell, turn.

Row 8: Ch 3, shell in ch sp of first shell, ch 3, sk next ch-3 sp, sc in next ch-4 sp, [ch 4, sc in next ch-4 sp] 8 times, ch 3, shell in ch sp of next shell, turn.

Row 9: Ch 3, shell in ch sp of first shell, ch 3, sk next ch-3 sp, sc in next ch-4 sp, [ch 4, sc in next ch-4 sp] 7 times, ch 3, shell in ch sp of next shell, turn.

Row 10: Ch 3, shell in ch sp of first shell, ch 3, sk next ch-3 sp, sc in next ch-4 sp, [ch 4, sc in next ch-4 sp] 6 times, ch 3, shell in ch sp of next shell, turn.

Row 11: Ch 3, shell in ch sp of first shell, ch 3, sk next ch-3 sp, sc in next ch-4 sp, [ch 4, sc in next ch-4 sp] 5 times, ch 3, shell in ch sp of next shell, turn.

Row 12: Ch 3, shell in ch sp first shell, ch 3, sk next ch-3 sp, sc in next ch-4 sp, [ch 4, sc in next ch-4 sp] 4 times, ch 3, shell in ch sp of next shell, turn.

Row 13: Ch 3, shell in ch sp of first shell, ch 3, sk next ch-3 sp, sc in next ch-4 sp, [ch 4, sc in next ch-4 sp] 3 times, ch 3, shell in ch sp of next shell, turn.

Row 14: Ch 3, shell in ch sp of first shell, ch 3, sk next ch-3 sp, sc in next ch-4 sp, [ch 4, sc in next ch-4 sp] twice, ch 3, shell in ch sp of next shell, turn.

Row 15: Ch 3, shell in ch sp of first shell, ch 3, sk next ch-3 sp, sc in next ch-4 sp, ch 4, sc in next ch-4 sp, ch 3, shell in ch sp of next shell, turn.

Row 16: Ch 3, shell in ch sp of first shell, ch 3, sc in next ch-4 sp, ch 3, shell in ch sp of next shell, turn.

Row 17: Ch 3, shell in ch sp of first shell, shell in ch sp of next shell. Fasten off.

Complete 2nd Inner Pineapple
Row 4: With RS facing, join in ch sp of next unworked shell on rnd 3, beg shell in same ch sp, ch 3, sk next ch-3 sp, tr in next dc, [ch 1, tr in next dc] 11 times, ch 3, shell in ch sp of next shell, turn.

Rows 5–17: Rep rows 5–17 of First Inner Pineapple, **do not fasten off** at end of row 17, turn.

Outer Section
Rnd 18: Now working in rnds, sl st in each of first 2 dc and in ch-2 sp, ch 1, sc in same ch sp, ch 7, sc in ch sp of next shell, *working down side of Pineapple, ch 7, sc in end of row 17, [ch 7, sk next row, sc in end of next row] 6 times, [ch 7, sc in next ch-7 sp] twice, ch 7, sc in top of end st of row 4, [ch 7, sk next row, sc in end of next row] 6 times**, [ch 7, sc in ch sp of next shell] twice, rep from * around, ending last rep at **, ch 7, join in beg sc.

Rnd 19: Sl st in each of next 4 chs, beg shell in same ch, ch 3, [shell in next ch-7 sp, ch 3] around, join in 3rd ch of beg ch-3. (36 shells)

Rnd 20: Sl st in next dc and in ch-2 sp, ch 1, sc in same ch sp, *ch 4, sc in next ch-3 sp, **picot** (see Special Stitches), ch 4**, sc in ch sp of next shell, rep from * around, ending last

36 Pineapples Through the Home • Annie's Attic • Berne, IN 46711 • DRGnetwork.com

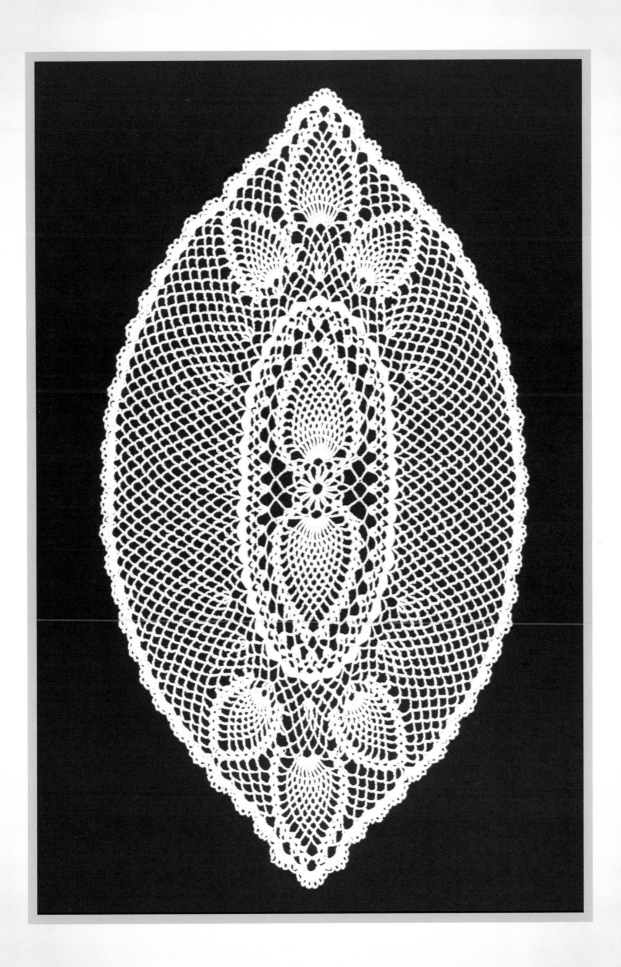

rep at **, join in beg sc.

Rnd 21: Sl st in each of next 2 chs, ch 1, sc in same ch sp, ch 5, [sc in next ch-4 sp, ch 5] around, join in beg sc. *(72 ch-5 sps)*

Rnd 22: Sl st in each of next 3 chs, ch 1, sc in same ch sp, [9 dc in next ch-5 sp, sc in next ch-5 sp] around, ending with 9 dc in last ch-5 sp, join in beg sc.

Rnd 23: Ch 1, sc in first sc, *ch 6, sk next 4 dc, sc in next dc, ch 6**, sc in next sc, rep from * around, ending last rep at **, join in beg sc.

Rnd 24: Sl st in each of next 3 chs, ch 1, sc in same ch sp, ch 6, [sc in next ch-6 sp, ch 6] around, join in beg sc. *(72 ch-6 sps)*

Rnd 25: Sl st in each of next 3 chs, ch 1, sc in same ch sp, ch 6, *(sc, ch 6) 3 times in next ch sp, [sc in next ch sp, ch 6] twice*, rep between * once, **(sc, ch 6) 3 times in next ch sp, [sc in next ch sp, ch 6] 17 times**, rep between * 6 times, rep between ** once, rep between * 3 times, (sc, ch 6) 3 times in next ch sp, sc in next ch sp, ch 6, join in beg sc. *(100 ch-6 sps)*

Rnd 26: Sl st in each of next 3 chs, ch 1, sc in same ch sp, [ch 6, sc in next ch-6 sp] around, ending with ch 2, tr in beg sc to form last ch-6 sp.

Rnd 27: Beg shell in ch sp just formed, ◊*ch 3, sc in next sp, 8 dc in next ch sp, sc in next ch sp, ch 3, shell in next ch sp, ch 3, sc in next ch sp*, [ch 6, sc in next ch sp] 34 times, ch 3, shell in next ch sp, rep between * once, [ch 6, sc in next ch sp] 4 times, ch 3◊◊, shell in next sp, rep from ◊ around, ending last rep at ◊◊, join in 3rd ch of beg ch-3.

Rnd 28: Sl st in next dc and in ch-2 sp, beg shell in same ch sp, ◊*ch 3, sc in next ch-3 sp, dc in next dc, [ch 1, dc in next dc] 7 times, sc in next ch-3 sp, ch 3, shell in ch sp of next shell, ch 6*, [sc in next ch-6 sp, ch 6] 34 times, shell in ch sp of next shell, rep between * once, [sc in next ch-6 sp, ch 6] 4 times◊◊, shell in ch sp of next shell, rep from ◊ around, ending last rep at ◊◊, join in 3rd ch of beg ch-3.

Rnd 29: Sl st in next dc and in ch-2 sp, beg shell in same ch sp, ◊*ch 3, sc in next dc, [ch 4, sc in next dc]

7 times, ch 3, shell in ch sp of next shell, ch 3, sc in next ch-6 sp*, [ch 6, sc in next ch-6 sp] 34 times, ch 3, shell in ch sp of next shell, rep between * once, [ch 6, sc in next ch-6 sp] 4 times, ch 3◊◊, shell in ch sp of next shell, rep from ◊ around, ending last rep at ◊◊, join in 3rd ch of beg ch-3.

Rnd 30: Sl st in next dc and in ch-2 sp, beg shell in same sp, ◊*ch 3, sk next ch-3 sp, sc in next ch-4 sp, [ch 4, sc in next ch-4 sp] 6 times, ch 3, shell in ch sp of next shell, ch 6, sk next ch-3 sp*, [sc in next ch-6 sp, ch 6] 34 times, shell in ch sp of next shell, rep between * once, [sc in next ch-6 sp, ch 6] 4 times◊◊, shell in ch sp of next shell, rep from ◊ around, ending last rep at ◊◊, join in 3rd ch of beg ch-3.

Rnd 31: Sl st in next dc and in ch-2 sp, beg shell in same ch sp, ◊*ch 3, sk next ch-3 sp, sc in next ch-4 sp, [ch 4, sc in next ch-4 sp] 5 times, ch 3, shell in ch sp of next shell*, ch 3, sc in next ch-6 sp, [ch 6, sc in next ch-6 sp] 34 times, ch 3, shell in ch sp of next shell, rep between * once, ch 1, shell in next ch-6 sp, ch 3, sc in next ch-6 sp, 10 dc in next ch-6 sp, sc in next ch-6 sp, ch 3, shell in next ch-6 sp, ch 1◊◊, shell in ch sp of next shell, rep from ◊ around, ending last rep at ◊◊, join in 3rd ch of beg ch-3.

Rnd 32: Sl st in next dc and in ch-2 sp, beg shell in same ch sp, ◊*ch 3, sk next ch-3 sp, sc in next ch-4 sp, [ch 4, sc in next ch-4 sp] 4 times ch 3, shell in ch sp of next shell*, ch 6, sk next ch-3 sp, [sc in next ch-6 sp, ch 6] 34 times, shell in ch sp of next shell, rep between * once, ch 2, shell in ch sp of next shell, ch 3, sk next ch-3 sp, tr in next dc, [ch 1, tr in next dc] 9 times, ch 3, shell in ch sp of next shell, ch 2◊◊, shell in ch sp of next shell, rep from ◊ around, ending last rep at ◊◊, join in 3rd ch of beg ch-3.

Rnd 33: Sl st in next dc and in ch-2 sp, beg shell in same ch sp, ◊*ch 3, sk next ch-3 sp, sc in next ch-4 sp, [ch 4, sc in next ch-4 sp] 3 times, ch 3, shell in ch sp of next shell, ch 6*, [sc in next ch-6 sp, ch 6] 35 times, shell in ch sp of next shell, rep between *

once, shell in ch sp of next shell, ch 3, sc in next tr, [ch 4, sc in next tr] 9 times, ch 3, shell in ch sp of next shell, ch 6◊◊, shell in ch sp of next shell, rep from ◊ around, ending last rep at ◊◊, join in 3rd ch of beg ch-3.

Rnd 34: Sl st in next dc and in ch-2 sp, beg shell in same ch sp, ◊*ch 3, sk next ch-3 sp, sc in next ch-4 sp, [ch 4, sc in next ch-4 sp] twice, ch 3, shell in ch sp of next shell, ch 6*, [sc in next ch-6 sp, ch 6] 36 times, shell in ch sp of next shell, rep between * once, sc in next ch-6 sp, ch 6, shell in ch sp of next shell, ch 3, sk next ch-3 sp, sc in next ch-4 sp, [ch 4, sc in next ch-4 sp] 8 times, ch 3, shell in ch sp of next shell, ch 6, sc in next ch-6 sp, ch 6◊◊, shell in ch sp of next shell, rep from ◊ around, ending last rep at ◊◊, join in 3rd ch of beg ch-3.

Rnd 35: Sl st in next dc and in ch-2 sp, beg shell in same ch sp, ◊*ch 3, sk next ch-3 sp, sc in next ch-4 sp, ch 4, sc in next ch-4 sp, ch 3, shell in ch sp of next shell, ch 6*, [sc in next ch-6 sp, ch 6] 37 times, shell in ch sp of next shell, rep between * once, [sc in next ch-6 sp, ch 6] twice, shell in ch sp of next shell, ch 3, sk next ch-3 sp, sc in next ch-4 sp, [ch 4, sc in next ch-4 sp] 7 times, ch 3, shell in ch sp of next shell, ch 6, [sc in next ch-6 sp, ch 6] twice◊◊, shell in ch sp of next shell, rep from ◊ around, ending last rep at ◊◊, join in 3rd ch of beg ch-3.

Rnd 36: Sl st in next dc and in ch-2 sp, beg shell in same sp, ◊*ch 3, sk next ch-3 sp, sc in next ch-4 sp, ch 3, shell in ch sp of next shell, ch 6*, [sc in next ch-6 sp, ch 6] 38 times, shell in ch sp of next shell, rep between * once, [sc in next ch-6 sp, ch 6] 3 times, shell in ch sp of next shell, ch 3, sk next ch-3 sp, sc in next ch-4 sp, [ch 4, sc in next ch-4 sp] 6 times, ch 3, shell in ch sp of next shell, ch 6, [sc in next ch-6 sp, ch 6] 3 times◊◊, shell in ch sp of next shell, rep from ◊ around, ending last rep at ◊◊, join in 3rd ch of beg ch-3.

Rnd 37: Sl st in next dc and in ch-2 sp, beg shell in same ch sp, shell in ch sp of next shell, *ch 6, [sc in next ch-6 sp, ch 6] 39 times, [shell in ch sp of next shell] twice, ch 6, [sc in next ch-6 sp, ch 6] 4 times, shell in ch sp of next shell, ch 3, sk next ch-3 sp, sc in next ch-4 sp, [ch 4, sc in next ch-4 sp] 5 times, ch 3, shell in ch sp of next shell, ch 6, [sc in next ch-6 sp, ch 6] 4 times**, [shell in ch sp of next shell] twice, rep from * around, ending last rep at **, join in 3rd ch of beg ch-3. Fasten off.

Complete First Outer Pineapple
Row 38: With RS facing, join in ch sp of first unworked shell on rnd 37 at right edge of center Pineapple on either end of Runner, beg shell in same ch sp, ch 3, sk next ch-3 sp, sc in next ch-4 sp, [ch 4, sc in next ch-4 sp] 4 times, ch 3, shell in ch sp of next shell, leaving rem sts unworked, turn.
Rows 39–43: Rep rows 13–17 of First Inner Pineapple.

Complete 2nd Outer Pineapple
Rows 38–43: On opposite end of Runner, rep rows 38–43 of First Outer Pineapple, **do not fasten off** at end of row 43, turn.

Edging
Rnd 1: Now working in rnds, sl st in next dc and in ch-2 sp, ch 1, sc in same sp, ch 6, sc in ch sp of next shell, *working down side of Pineapple, ch 6, sc in end of row 17, [ch 6, sk next row, sc in end of next row] twice, [ch 6, sc in next ch-6 sp] 5 times, ch 6, sc in ch sp of each of next 2 shells, [ch 6, sc in next ch-6 sp] 40 times, ch 6, sc in ch sp of each of next 2 shells, [ch 6, sc in next ch-6 sp] 5 times, ch 6, sc in top of end st or row 38, [ch 6, sk next row, sc over beg ch-3 of

next row] twice*, [ch 6, sc in ch sp of next shell] twice, rep between * once, ch 6, join in beg sc.
Rnd 2: Sl st in next ch-6 sp, ch 3, 14 dc in same ch sp, sc in next ch sp, picot, *[11 dc in next sp, sc in next ch sp, picot] 4 times, [9 dc in next ch sp, sc in next ch sp, picot] 21 times, *[11 dc in next sp, sc in next ch sp, picot] 4 times, 15 dc in next ch sp, sc in next ch sp, picot, rep from * around, join in 3rd ch of beg ch-3.
Rnd 3: Working in **back lps** (see Stitch Guide) only, sl st in next dc, ch 1, sc

in same st, sk next dc, next picot and next dc, ◊*[ch 3, sk next dc, sc in next dc] 6 times, **ch 3, sk next dc, next picot and next dc, sc in next dc, [ch 3, sk next dc, sc in next dc] 4 times, rep from * 3 times**, ***ch 3, sk next dc, next picot and next dc, sc in next dc, [ch 3, sk next dc, sc in next dc] 3 times, rep from *** 20 times, rep between **, ch 3, sk next dc, next picot and next dc, sc in next dc, rep from ◊ around, ending with ch 3, sk next dc, next picot and next dc, join in beg sc. Fasten off. ❑❑

Pineapple Rug

Design by Agnes Russell

SKILL LEVEL

INTERMEDIATE

FINISHED SIZE
29 inches in diameter, excluding Fringe

MATERIALS
- ❑ Size 10 crochet cotton (350 yds per ball):
  5 balls color of choice
- ❑ Size H/8/5mm crochet hook or size needed to obtain gauge

GAUGE
With 5 strands crochet cotton held tog: Rnds 1–5 = 4½ inches; 4 shells = 3 inches

PATTERN NOTES
Join with slip stitch as indicated unless otherwise stated.

Chain-2 at beginning of row or round counts as first double crochet unless otherwise stated.

SPECIAL STITCHES
Beginning shell (beg shell): Ch 3, (dc, ch 2, 2 dc) in place indicated.

Shell: (2 dc, ch 2, 2 dc) in place indicated.

If row or rnd begs with shell, simply sl st in to ch-2 sp and work beg shell in same ch sp.

INSTRUCTIONS
RUG
Rnd 1: Holding 5 strands of crochet cotton tog, ch 5, sl st in first ch to form ring, ch 1, 12 sc in ring, **join** (see Pattern Notes) in beg sc. (12 sc)

Rnd 2: Ch 1, sc in first st, 2 sc in next st, [sc in next st, 2 sc in next st] around, join in beg sc. (18 sc)

Rnd 3: Ch 2 (see Pattern Notes), dc in same st, 2 dc in each st around, join in 2nd ch of beg ch-2. (36 dc)

Rnd 4: Ch 1, sc in each of first 5 sts, 2 sc in next st, [sc in each of next 5 sts, 2 sc in next st] around, join in beg sc. (42 sc)

Rnd 5: Ch 1, sc in each of first 6 sts, 2 sc in next st, [sc in each of next 6 sts, 2 sc in next st] around, join in beg sc. (48 sc)

Rnd 6: [Ch 3, sk next st, sl st in next st] around, join in first ch of beg ch-3. (24 ch-3 sps)

Rnd 7: Sl st in center of next ch-3 sp, ch 3, [sl st in next ch-3 sp, ch 3] around, ending with sl st in same st as beg ch-3.

Rnd 8: Ch 1, 3 sc in each ch-3 sp around, join in beg sc. (72 sc)

Rnd 9: Ch 2, dc in same st, dc in next st, [2 dc in next st, dc in next st] around, join in 2nd ch of beg ch-2. (108 dc)

Rnd 10: Ch 1, sc in first st, sc in each st around, join in beg sc.

Rnd 11: Rep rnd 10.

Rnds 12 & 13: Rep rnds 6 and 7. (54 ch-3 sps)

Rnd 14: Ch 1, 2 sc in each ch-3 sp around, join in beg sc. (108 dc)

Rnd 15: Beg shell (see Special Stitches) in first st, ch 1, sk next 3 sts, [**shell** (see Special Stitches) in next st, ch 1, sk next 3 sts] around, join in 3rd ch of beg ch-3. (27 shells)

Rnd 16: [Shell in ch sp of next shell, ch 1, 8 dc in ch sp of next shell, ch 1, shell in ch sp of next shell, ch 1] around, join in 3rd ch of beg ch-3. (18 shells, 9 pineapple bases)

Rnd 17: *Shell in ch sp of next shell, ch 1, dc in first dc of next 8-dc group, [ch 1, dc in next dc] 7 times, ch 1, shell in ch sp of next shell, ch 1, rep from * around, join in 3rd ch of beg ch-3.

Rnd 18: *Shell in ch sp of next shell, ch 1, sk next ch-1 sp, sc in next ch-1 sp between first 2 dc of pineapple, [ch 3, sc in next ch-1 sp] 6 times, ch 1, shell in ch sp of next shell, ch 1, rep from * around, join in 3rd ch of beg ch-3.

Rnd 19: *Shell in ch sp of next shell, ch 1, sc in next ch-3 sp, [ch 3, sc in next ch-3 sp] 5 times, ch 1, shell in ch sp of next shell, ch 1, rep from * around, join in 3rd ch of beg ch-3.

Rnd 20: *Shell in ch sp of next shell, ch 1, sc in next ch-3 sp, [ch 3, sc in next ch-3 sp] 4 times, ch 1, shell in ch sp of next shell, ch 1, dc in ch-1 sp between shells, ch 1, rep from * around, join in 3rd ch of beg ch-3.

Rnd 21: *Shell in ch sp of next shell, ch 1, sc in next ch-3 sp, [ch 3, sc in next ch-3 sp] 3 times, ch 1, shell in ch sp of next shell, ch 1, sk next ch-1 sp, 3 dc in single dc between shells, ch 1, rep from * around, join in 3rd ch of beg ch-3.

Rnd 22: *Shell in ch sp of next shell, ch 1, sc in next ch-3 sp, [ch 3, sc in next ch-3 sp] twice, ch 1, shell in ch sp of next shell, ch 1, sk next ch-1 sp, working across the 3-dc between shells, 2 dc in next dc, 1 dc in next dc, 2 dc in next dc, ch 1, rep from * around, join in 3rd ch of beg ch-3.

Rnd 23: [Shell in ch sp of next shell, ch 1, sc in next ch-3 sp, ch 3, sc in next ch-3 sp, ch 1, shell in ch sp of next shell, ch 1, sk next ch-1 sp, 2 dc in next dc, dc in each of next 3 dc, 2 dc in next dc, ch 1] around, join in 3rd ch of beg ch-3.

Rnd 24: [Shell in ch sp of next shell, ch 1, dc in ch-3 sp of pineapple, ch 1, shell in ch sp of next shell, ch 1, sk ch-1 sp, 2 dc in next dc, dc in each of next 5 dc, 2 dc in next dc, ch 1] around, join in 3rd ch of beg ch-3.

Rnd 25: Sl st in ch sp of shell, ch 1, *sc in ch-1 sp of shell, [ch 3, sc in next ch-1 sp] twice, ch 3, sc in ch-1 sp of next shell, ch 3, sc in next ch-1 sp, [ch 3, sk next dc, sc in next dc] 4 times, ch 3, sc in next ch-1 sp, ch 3, rep from * around, join in beg sc. (90 ch-3 sps)

Rnd 26: Sl st in next ch-3 sp, ch 1, sc in same ch-3 sp, ch 3, [sc in next ch-3 sp, ch 3] around, join in beg sc.

Rnd 27: Rep rnd 8. (270 sc)

Rnds 28–31: Rep rnd 10.

Rnd 32: [Ch 3, sk next st, sl st in next st] around. (135 ch-3 sps)

Rnd 33: Sl st in next ch-3 sp, [ch 3, sl st in next ch-3 sp] around. Fasten off.

Finishing

On padded surface, with WS of Rug facing, steam-press Rug.

Fringe

Cut 8 strands each 10 inches in length. Holding all strands tog, fold in half, pull fold through, pull ends through fold. Pull to tighten.

Attach Fringe in each ch-3 sp around rnd 33.

Cut 18-inch length of ribbon, weave through ch-3 sps of rnd 6, securing ends on WS.

Cut 1 yd length of ribbon, weave through ch-3 sps of rnd 12, securing ends on WS.

Weave rem 3 yd length of ribbon through ch-3 sps of rnd 32, beg and ending on RS, tie ends in a bow. ❏❏

Designs by Agnes Russell

SKILL LEVEL

INTERMEDIATE

FINISHED SIZE

2¾ inches wide, fits standard pillowcases and full-size sheets

MATERIALS

- ❑ Size 10 crochet cotton: 700 yds
- ❑ Size 8/1.50mm steel crochet hook or size needed to obtain gauge
- ❑ Sewing needle
- ❑ Matching sewing thread
- ❑ Set of standard size pillowcases
- ❑ Full-size flat sheet
- ❑ 5⅛ yds 5mm-wide blue picot edged ribbon

GAUGE

4 shells = 1 inch

SPECIAL STITCHES

Double shell: (2 dc, {ch 2, 2 dc} twice) in place indicated.

Shell: (2 dc, ch 2, 2 dc) in place indicated.

INSTRUCTIONS
PILLOWCASE EDGING

Row 1 (WS): Ch 14, (dc, ch 2, 2 dc) in 4th ch from hook *(first 3 chs count as first dc)*, ch 2, sk next 4 chs, **double shell** *(see Special Stitches)* in next ch, ch 2, sk next 4 chs, **shell** *(see Special Stitches)* in next ch, turn. *(2 shells, 1 double shell)*

Row 2 (RS): Ch 3, shell in ch sp of next shell, ch 2, shell in ch sp of each of next 2 shells, ch 2, shell in ch sp of next shell, turn. *(4 shells)*

Row 3 (WS): Ch 3, shell in ch sp of next shell, [ch 2, shell in ch sp of next shell] 3 times, turn.

Row 4 (RS): Ch 3, [shell in ch sp of next shell, ch 2] twice, 8 dc in next

ch-2 sp of next shell, ch 2, shell in ch sp of next shell, turn. *(3 shells, 1 pineapple base)*

Row 5: Ch 3, shell in ch sp of next shell, ch 2, dc in first dc of next 8-dc group, [ch 1, dc in next dc] 7 times, [ch 2, shell in ch sp of next shell] twice, turn.

Row 6: Ch 3, [shell in ch sp of next shell, ch 2] twice, sc in next ch-1 sp, [ch 3, sc in next ch-1 sp] 6 times, ch 2, shell in ch sp of next shell, turn.

Row 7: Ch 3, shell in ch sp of next shell, ch 2, sc in next ch-3 sp, [ch 3, sc in next ch-3 sp] 5 times, [ch 2, shell in ch sp of next shell] twice, turn.

Row 8: Ch 3, [shell in ch sp of next shell, ch 2] twice, sc in next ch-3 sp, [ch 3, sc in next ch-3 sp] 4 times, ch 2, shell in ch sp of next shell, turn.

Row 9: Ch 3, shell in ch sp of next shell, ch 2, sc in next ch-3 sp, [ch 3, sc in next ch-3 sp] 3 times, [ch 2, shell in ch sp of next shell] twice, turn.

Row 10: Ch 3, [shell in ch sp of next shell, ch 2] twice, sc in next ch-3 sp, [ch 3, sc in next ch-3 sp] twice, ch 2, shell in ch sp of next shell, turn.

Row 11: Ch 3, shell in ch sp of next shell, ch 2, sc in next ch-3 sp, ch 3, sc in next ch-3 sp, [ch 2, shell in ch sp of next shell] twice, turn.

Row 12: Ch 3, [shell in ch sp of next shell, ch 2] twice, ch 2, sc in next ch-3 sp, ch 2, shell in ch sp of next shell, turn.

Row 13: Ch 3, shell in ch sp of next shell, ch 2, double shell in ch sp of next shell, ch 2, shell in ch sp of next shell, turn.

Rows 14–109: [Rep rows 2–13 consecutively] 8 times.

Rows 110–119: Rep rows 2–11. *(10 pineapples at end of last row)*

Row 120: Ch 3, *2 dc in ch-2 sp of shell, ch 1, sl st in opposite side of starting ch at base of shell, ch 1, 2

dc in same ch-2 sp of shell on row 119*, ch 2, rep between * once, ch 2, sc in next ch-3 sp, ch 2, rep between * once. Fasten off.

The joining of row 120 to opposite side of foundation ch of row 1 is the seam and, when joined, will be positioned over pillowcase seam.

Finishing

Steam-press edging, starch lightly if desired.

Cut 48 inches of ribbon. For desired positioning of bow, start weaving ribbon at any row 12 of crocheted edging. Weave ribbon over and under the ch-2 sps between shells around edging, tie ends in a bow.

Matching seams, place crocheted edging over pillowcase, pin edging in place so that sewn hem of case is not visible. Sew ch-3 lps and shells next to ribbon to case.

SHEET EDGING

Rows 1–13: Rep rows 1–13 of Pillowcase Edging.

Rows 14–229: [Rep rows 2–13 consecutively] 18 times.

Rows 230–240: Rep rows 2–12 once.

Row 241: Ch 3, shell in ch sp of each of next 2 shells, ch 2, shell in ch sp of next shell. Fasten off.

Finishing

Steam-press edging, starch lightly if desired.

Cut 90 inches of ribbon. Weave over and under ch-2 sps between shells across Edging. Turn ends under to WS and secure.

Place sheet on flat surface. Pin edging in place so that sewn hem of sheet is not visible. Sew ch-3 lps and shells next to ribbon to sheet.

Sew rows 1 and 241 of Edging to sheet. ❑❑

Island Ecstasy Runner

Design by Jo Ann Maxwell

FINISHED SIZE
9¾ x 25½ inches

MATERIALS
- ❑ Size 10 crochet cotton:
  500 yds ecru
- ❑ Size 5/1.90mm steel crochet
  hook or size needed to
  obtain gauge
- ❑ Craft glue

GAUGE
15 dc = 2 inches
Each strip = ⅜-inch-wide

PATTERN NOTES
Join with slip stitch as indicated unless
otherwise stated.

Chain-3 at beginning of row or round
counts as first double crochet unless
otherwise stated.

SPECIAL STITCHES
Picot: Ch 3, sl st in last sc.

Beginning shell (beg shell): Ch 3
(see Pattern Notes), (dc, ch 2, 2 dc)
in place indicated.

Shell: (2 dc, ch 2, 2 dc) in place
indicated.

INSTRUCTIONS

LONG STRIP
Make 6.
Ch 100, dc in 4th ch from hook *(first
3 chs count as first dc)* and in each
ch across. Fasten off.

SHORT STRIP
Make 11.
Ch 50, dc in 4th ch from hook *(first 3
chs count as first dc)* and in each ch
across. Fasten off.

RUNNER
Rnd 1: Working in end of each Long
Strip, join with sc in end of first Long
Strip, 2 sc in same place, ch 7, [3 sc in
end of next Long Strip, ch 7] 5 times,
weave Short Strips through Long
Strips according to Strip Diagram
(see Fig. 1), working in ends of Short
and Long Strips, [3 sc in end of next
Short Strip or next Long Strip, ch 7]
around, **join** *(see Pattern Notes)* in
first sc. *(34 ch-7 sps)*

Rnd 2: Sl st in next st, ch 1, sc in same
st, **picot** *(see Special Stitches),* *ch 1,
sk first ch of next ch-7, 2 dc in each
of next 2 chs, dc in next ch, 2 dc in
each of next 2 chs, ch 1, sk next ch**,
(sc, picot) in center st of next 3-sc
group, rep from * around, ending
last rep at **, join in first sc.

Rnd 3: Working in front of picot, sl st

in next ch, sl st in each of next 4 dc,
ch 3 *(see Pattern Notes),* **shell** *(see
Special Stitches)* in next dc, dc in next
dc, ch 5, sk next 6 dc and picot, [dc in
next dc, shell in next dc, dc in next dc,
ch 5, sk next 6 dc and picot] around,
join in 3rd ch of beg ch-3.

Rnd 4: Ch 3, dc in each of next 2 sts,
◊*3 dc in next ch-2 sp, dc in each of
next 3 sts, sc in next ch-5 sp*, [ch 2,
sk next 2 sts, dc in next st, shell in
next ch-2 sp, dc in next st, ch 2, sc
in next ch-5 sp] 3 times, dc in each
of next 3 sts, rep between * once, [ch
2, sk next 2 sts, dc in next st, shell in
next ch-2 sp, dc in next st, ch 2, sc
in next ch-5 sp 12 times◊, dc in each
of next 3 sts, rep between ◊ once,
join in 3rd ch of beg ch-3.

Rnd 5: Ch 4, dc in next dc, [ch 1, dc
in next dc] 7 times, ◊*sc in next ch-2
sp, ch 3, sk next 2 dc, dc in next dc,
shell in next ch-2 sp, dc in next dc*,
[ch 5, sk next 2 ch-2 sps, sk next 2
dc, dc in next dc, shell in next ch-2
sp, dc in next dc] twice, ch 3, sc in
next ch-2 sp, dc in next dc, [ch 1,
dc in next dc] 8 times, rep between
* once, ch 3, [sk next 2 ch-2 sps, dc
in each of next 3 dc, 3 dc in next
ch-2 sp, dc in each of next 3 dc] 10
times, ch 3, sk next 2 ch-2 sps, sk
next 2 dc, dc in next dc, shell in next
ch-2 sp, dc in next dc, ch 3, sc in

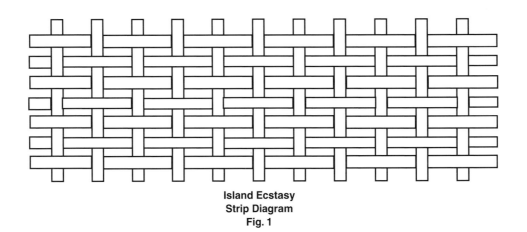

Island Ecstasy
Strip Diagram
Fig. 1

next ch-2 sp◊, dc in next dc, [ch 1, dc in next dc] 8 times, rep between ◊ once, join in 3rd ch of beg ch-4. Fasten off.

First End

Row 6: Now working in rows, join in 2nd dc of last shell, ch 3, *shell in next ch-2 sp, dc in next dc, ch 3, sk next ch-3 sp, sk next sc, sc in next dc, [ch 3, sc in next dc] 8 times, ch 3, sk next ch-3 sp, sk next 2 dc, dc in next dc, shell in next ch-2 sp, dc in next dc*, ch 3, sc in next ch-5 sp, dc in each of next 3 dc, 5 dc in next ch-2 sp, dc in each of next 3 dc, sc in next ch-5 sp, ch 3, sk next 2 dc, dc in next dc, rep between * once, leaving rem sts unworked, turn.

Row 7: Ch 3, sk next dc, *dc in next dc, shell in next ch-2 sp, dc in next dc, ch 3, sk next ch-3 sp, sc in next ch-3 sp, [ch 3, sc in next ch-3 sp] 7 times, ch 3, sk next ch-3 sp, sk next 2 dc, dc in next dc, shell in next ch-2 sp, dc in next dc*, ch 3, sc in next ch-3 sp, dc in next dc, [ch 1, dc in next dc] 10 times, sc in next ch-3 sp, ch 3, sk next 2 dc, rep between * once, turn.

Row 8: Ch 3, sk next dc, *dc in next dc, shell in next ch-2 sp, dc in next dc, ch 3, sk next ch-3 sp, sc in next ch-3 sp, [ch 3, sc in next ch-3 sp] 6 times, ch 3, sk next ch-3 sp, sk next 2 dc, dc in next dc, shell in next ch-2 sp, dc in next dc*, ch 3, sk next ch-3 sp, sk next sc, sc in next dc, [ch 3, sc in next dc] 10 times, ch 3, sk next sc, sk next ch-3 sp, sk next 2 dc, rep between * once, turn.

Row 9: Ch 3, sk next dc, dc in next dc, shell in next ch-2 sp, *dc in next dc, ch 3, sk next ch-3 sp, sc in next ch-3 sp, [ch 3, sc in next ch-3 sp] 5 times, ch 3, sk next ch-3 sp, sk next 2 dc, dc in next dc*, (2 dc, ch 2, 3 dc, ch 2, 2 dc) in next ch-2 sp, dc in next dc, ch 3, sk next ch-3 sp, sc in next ch-3 sp, [ch 3, sc in next ch-3 sp] 9 times, ch 3, sk next ch-3 sp, sk next 2 dc, dc in next dc, (2 dc, ch 2, 3 dc, ch 2, 2 dc) in next ch-2 sp, rep between * once, shell in next ch-2 sp, dc in next dc, turn.

Row 10: Ch 3, sk next st, dc in next dc, shell in next ch-2 sp, dc in next dc, ch 3, sk next ch-3 sp, sc in next ch-3 sp, **[ch 3, sc in next ch-3 sp] 4

times, *ch 3, sk next ch-3 sp, sk next 2 dc, dc in next dc, shell in next ch-2 sp, dc in next dc**, ch 1, sk next dc, dc in next dc, shell in next ch-2 sp, dc in next dc, ch 3, sk next ch-3 sp, sc in next ch-3 sp*, [ch 3, sc in next ch-3 sp] 8 times, rep between * once, rep between ** once, turn.

First Pineapple

Row 11: Ch 3, sk next dc, dc in next dc, shell in next ch-2 sp, dc in next dc, ch 3, sk next ch-3 sp, sc in next ch-3 sp, [ch 3, sc in next ch-3 sp] 3 times, ch 3, sk next ch-3 sp, sk next 2 dc, dc in next dc, shell in next ch-2 sp, dc in next dc leaving rem sts unworked, turn.

Row 12: Ch 3, sk next dc, dc in next dc, shell in next ch-2 sp, dc in next dc, ch 3, sk next ch-3 sp, sc in next ch-3 sp, [ch 3, sc in next ch-3 sp] twice, ch 3, sk next ch-3 sp, sk next 2 dc, dc in next dc, shell in next ch-2 sp, dc in next dc, turn.

Row 13: Ch 3, sk next dc, dc in next dc, shell in next ch-2 sp, dc in next dc, ch 3, sk next ch-3 sp, [sc in next ch-3 sp, ch 3] 2 times, sk next ch-3 sp, sk next 2 dc, dc in next dc, shell in next ch-2 sp, dc in next dc, turn.

Row 14: Ch 3, sk next dc, dc in next dc, shell in next ch-2 sp, dc in next dc, ch 3, sk next ch-3 sp, sc in next ch-3 sp, ch 3, sk next ch-3 sp, sk next 2 dc, dc in next dc, shell in next ch-2 sp, dc in next dc, turn.

Row 15: Ch 3, sk next dc, dc in next dc, shell in next ch-2 sp, dc in next dc, sk next 2 ch-3 sps, sk next 2 dc, dc in next dc, shell in next ch-2 sp, dc in next dc. Fasten off.

Center Pineapple

Row 11: Sk next 4 sts and next ch-1 sp on row 10, join with sl st in next dc, ch 3, shell in next ch-2 sp, dc in next dc, ch 3, sk next ch-3 sp, sc in next ch-3 sp, [ch 3, sc in next ch-3 sp] 7 times, ch 3, sk next ch-3 sp, sk next 2 dc, dc in next dc, shell in next ch-2 sp, dc in next dc, leaving rem sts unworked, turn.

Row 12: Ch 3, sk next dc, dc in next dc, shell in next ch-2 sp, dc in next dc, ch 3, sk next ch-3 sp, sc in next ch-3 sp, [ch 3, sc in next ch-3 sp] 6 times, ch 3, sk next ch-3 sp, sk next

2 dc, dc in next dc, shell in next ch-2 sp, dc in next dc, turn.

Row 13: Ch 3, sk next dc, dc in next dc, shell in next ch-2 sp, dc in next dc, ch 3, sk next ch-3 sp, sc in next ch-3 sp, [ch 3, sc in next ch-3 sp] 5 times, ch 3, sk next ch-3 sp, sk next 2 dc, dc in next dc, shell in next ch-2 sp, dc in next dc, turn.

Row 14: Ch 3, sk next dc, dc in next dc, shell in next ch-2 sp, dc in next dc, ch 3, sk next ch-3 sp, sc in next ch-3 sp, [ch 3, sc in next ch-3 sp] 4 times, ch 3, sk next ch-3 sp, sk next 2 dc, dc in next dc, shell in next ch-2 sp, dc in next dc, turn.

Row 15: Ch 3, sk next dc, dc in next dc, shell in next ch-2 sp, dc in next dc, ch 3, sk next ch-3 sp, sc in next ch-3 sp, [ch 3, sc in next ch-3 sp] 3 times, ch 3, sk next ch-3 sp, sk next 2 dc, dc in next dc, shell in next ch-2 sp, dc in next dc, turn.

Rows 16–19: Rep rows 12–15 of First Pineapple.

Last Pineapple

Row 11: Sk next 4 sts and next ch-1 sp on row 10, join with sl st in next st, ch 3, shell in next ch-2 sp, dc in next st, ch 3, sk next ch-3 sp, sc in next ch-3 sp, [ch 3, sc in next ch-3 sp] 3 times, ch 3, sk next ch-3 sp, sk next 2 sts, dc in next st, shell in next ch-2 sp, dc in next st, turn.

Rows 12–15: Rep rows 12–15 of First Pineapple.

2nd Side

Row 6: Now working in rows, join in 2nd st of next shell on rnd 5 on opposite end of Runner, rep row 1 of First Side.

Rows 7–10: Rep rows 7–10 of First Side.

First Pineapple

Rows 11–15: Work same as First Side First Pineapple.

Center Pineapple

Rows 11–19: Work same as First Side Center Pineapple.

Last Pineapple

Rows 11–15: Work same as First Side Last Pineapple.

If desired, glue Strips tog at each overlap. ❏❏

Stitch Guide

ABBREVIATIONS

beg	begin/beginning
bpdc	back post double crochet
bpsc	back post single crochet
bptr	back post treble crochet
CC	contrasting color
ch	chain stitch
ch-	refers to chain or space previously made (i.e., ch-1 space)
ch sp	chain space
cl	cluster
cm	centimeter(s)
dc	double crochet
dec	decrease/decreases/decreasing
dtr	double treble crochet
fpdc	front post double crochet
fpsc	front post single crochet
fptr	front post treble crochet
g	gram(s)
hdc	half double crochet
inc	increase/increases/increasing
lp(s)	loop(s)
MC	main color
mm	millimeter(s)
oz	ounce(s)
pc	popcorn
rem	remain/remaining
rep	repeat(s)
rnd(s)	round(s)
RS	right side
sc	single crochet
sk	skip(ped)
sl st	slip stitch
sp(s)	space(s)
st(s)	stitch(es)
tog	together
tr	treble crochet
trtr	triple treble
WS	wrong side
yd(s)	yard(s)
yo	yarn over

Chain—ch: Yo, pull through lp on hook.

Slip stitch—sl st: Insert hook in st, yo, pull through both lps on hook.

Single crochet—sc: Insert hook in st, yo, pull through st, yo, pull through both lps on hook.

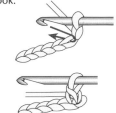

Front loop—front lp
Back loop—back lp

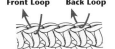

Front post stitch—fp:
Back post stitch—bp: When working post st, insert hook from right to left around post st on previous row.

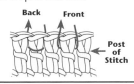

Half double crochet—hdc: Yo, insert hook in st, yo, pull through st, yo, pull through all 3 lps on hook.

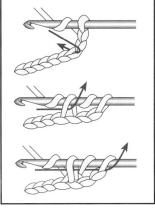

Double crochet—dc: Yo, insert hook in st, yo, pull through st, [yo, pull through 2 lps] twice.

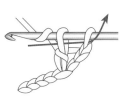

Change colors: Drop first color; with 2nd color, pull through last 2 lps of st.

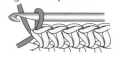

Treble crochet—tr: Yo 2 times, insert hook in st, yo, pull through st, [yo, pull through 2 lps] 3 times.

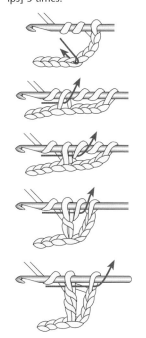

Double treble crochet—dtr: Yo 3 times, insert hook in st, yo, pull through st, [yo, pull through 2 lps] 4 times.

Single crochet decrease (sc dec): (Insert hook, yo, draw up a lp) in each of the sts indicated, yo, draw through all lps on hook.

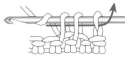

Example of 2-sc dec

Half double crochet decrease (hdc dec): (Yo, insert hook, yo, draw lp through) in each of the sts indicated, yo, draw through all lps on hook.

Double crochet decrease (dc dec): (Yo, insert hook, yo, draw lp through, yo, draw through 2 lps on hook) in each of the sts indicated, yo, draw through all lps on hook.

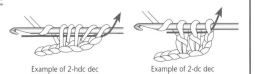

Example of 2-hdc dec   Example of 2-dc dec

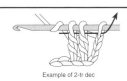

Example of 2-tr dec

Treble crochet decrease (tr dec): Holding back last lp of each st, tr in each of the sts indicated, yo, pull through all lps on hook.

US		UK
sl st (slip stitch)	=	sc (single crochet)
sc (single crochet)	=	dc (double crochet)
hdc (half double crochet)	=	htr (half treble crochet)
dc (double crochet)	=	tr (treble crochet)
tr (treble crochet)	=	dtr (double treble crochet)
dtr (double treble crochet)	=	ttr (triple treble crochet)
skip	=	miss

For more complete information, visit
FreePatterns.com

TOLL-FREE ORDER LINE or to request a free catalog (800) LV-ANNIE (800) 582-6643
Customer Service (800) AT-ANNIE (800) 282-6643, **Fax** (800) 882-6643
Visit anniesattic.com

We have made every effort to ensure the accuracy and completeness of these instructions.
We cannot, however, be responsible for human error, typographical mistakes or variations in individual work.

ISBN: 978-1-59635-204-9

Printed in USA   1 2 3 4 5 6 7 8 9